LEADING STUDENTS
INTO SCRIPTURE

SR. MARY KATHLEEN GLAVICH, SND

LEADING STUDENTS INTO SCRIPTURE

TWENTY-THIRD PUBLICATIONS
Mystic, Connecticut

ACKNOWLEDGMENTS

"Israel's Greatest King" (Illustration B) is adapted from its original form in *God Loves His People* from the CHRIST OUR LIFE series written by the Sisters of Notre Dame and published by Loyola University Press.

The modern version of Psalm 23 (p. 20), the crossword puzzle (pp. 92-94), and the original form of "Queen Esther" (p. 69) appeared in *Called by the Father*, Teacher's Manual and Resource Book written by Sr. M. Kathleen Glavich, SND, and Sr. Loretta Pastva, SND, from the *Light of the World* series published by Benziger Publishing Co.

"Jonah, Patron of Catechists" (pp. 59-62) first appeared in *Catechist* magazine, September 1982, and is reprinted here by persmission of the publisher, Peter Li, Inc., 2451 E. River Rd., Dayton, OH 45439.

Unless otherwise noted, Scripture texts used in this work are taken from *The New American Bible*, copyright © 1970, by the Confraternity of Christian Doctrine, Washington, D.C., and are used by permission of the copyright owner. All rights reserved.

Scripture texts marked JB are taken from *The Jerusalem Bible*, copyright © 1966, Darton, Longman and Todd, Ltd., and Doubleday & Company, Inc., and are used by permission of the publisher.

Special thanks to Sr. Rita Mary Harwood, SND, Sr. Melannie Svoboda, SND, Sr. Mary David Horan, SND, Sr. Mary Martha Maynard, SND, and the other sisters in my community who encouraged me to give the talk at an NCEA convention which led to this book.

I am also grateful to Sr. Regina Marie Alfonso, SND, Sr. Mary Sheila Keily, SND, Don Curran, and Millie Sussman for their assistance.

The illustrations on pages 7, 13, 14, 16, 20, 22, 28, 30, 38, 43, 51, and 55 are all taken from Scripture-based sound filmstrips published by Twenty-Third Publications.

Second printing   September 1987

Twenty-Third Publications
P.O. Box 180
Mystic, CT 06355
(203) 536-2611

Library of Congress Catalog Card Number 86-51613
ISBN 0-89622-328-0

Cover by William Baker
Interior design by Andrea Carey
Edited by Gwen Costello

This book is dedicated to the catechists of the church who share the Good News with patience, perseverance, and love. May this Word of God be fulfilled in them:

"You will shine in the world like bright stars because you are offering it the word of life."
(Philippians 2:15-16 JB)

Contents

APPENDIX OF ILLUSTRATIONS

LEADING STUDENTS INTO SCRIPTURE

"Faith is contagious. As a believing Christian, you have more impact on your students than any textbook series or audiovisual could ever have. It's no surprise then that a key technique in teaching Scripture is personal sharing. Be willing to share what the Bible means to you."

Introduction

Lord, help me to lead my students into Scripture in such a way that they make the prayer of Jeremiah their own: "When I found your words, I devoured them; / they became my joy and the happiness of my heart" (Jeremiah 15:16).

This is a perfect prayer for catechists, for by leading our students into Scripture, we carry on the Christian mission in the spirit of Christ and the first Christians. When Jesus met the two disciples on the way to Emmaus, it was through Scripture that he taught them about himself (Luke 24:27). When Philip encountered the Ethiopian reading Isaiah, he asked, "Do you really grasp what you are reading?" The man replied, "How can I unless someone explains it to me?" Philip then proceeded to announce the Good News based on the text the man was reading. The Ethiopian was baptized and went on his way rejoicing (Acts 8:29-39). When we introduce our students to God's Word and teach them its meaning, we, too, are apostles spreading the Good News.

What Is the Bible?

• The Bible is the Word of God in the words of human beings, "living and effective, sharper than any two-edged sword" (Hebrews 4:12).

• It is a mirror that reflects ourselves and our human race, our grandeur and our folly.

• It is a communication system tuned in to God for directions as we journey to our promised land. "All scripture is inspired by God and can profitably be used for teaching, for refuting error, for guiding people's lives and leading them to be holy" (2 Timothy 3:16 JB).

• It is a love letter in which we are reassured by God that we are loved and can be saved. It has been called "a book drenched in love."

• It is a springboard for prayer, for dialogue with God who speaks through it. *The Constitution on Divine Revelation* states, "In the sacred books the Father who is in heaven comes lovingly to meet his children, and talks with them" (21).

• Most significantly, the Bible is a good way to know Jesus, for as Cardinal John Henry Newman wrote:

> . . .while the thought of Christ is but a creation of our minds, it may gradually be changed or fade away, it may become defective or perverted; whereas when we contemplate Christ as manifested in the Gospels, . . .then we shall at length believe in him with a conviction, a confidence, and an entireness, which can no more be annihilated than the belief in our senses.
>
> *(Parochial and Plain Sermons III, pg. 131)*

Jesus himself makes familiarity with God's Word and obedience to it essential for anyone who desires a relationship with him:

> If you make my word your home
> you will indeed be my disciples.
> You will learn the truth
> and the truth shall make you free *(John 8:31-32 JB)*.

And again, "My mother and my brothers are those who hear the Word of God and put it into practice" (Luke 8:21 JB).

Why Is It Important to Teach Students Scripture?

• Students need to become familiar with the Bible so that all their lives they do not think that Jesus cured leopards instead of lepers, or that an epistle is the wife of an apostle. Bible illiteracy prevents many Catholic adults from turning to Scripture for information, inspiration, or guidance. We can help our students, the next generation of adults, to read the Bible and to recognize it as God's Word.

• Students need to understand the real truth behind the stories of the Bible so that when they discover that many of them were not meant to be interpreted literally, they will not discard belief in God along with belief in the stories.

• Young Catholics today are often helpless when they deal with persons who quote Scripture liberally to evangelize or proselytize them.

• Our children thirst for an encounter with God that will give meaning and joy to their lives; that encounter can happen through Scripture.

• As we pray and reflect on Scripture, we imitate Mary, our Mother, the first and best disciple of the Lord. Mary teaches us to treasure God's words and actions and to ponder them in our hearts.

How Will This Book Help?

If you are reading this page, chances are you are already convinced of the value of Scripture and the need for leading students into its riches. You are probably looking for ways to teach the Bible. This book will help you plan scriptural activities that are effective and at the same time enjoyable. It will help you add variety to your plans and forestall those words that make a teacher's heart sink: "This is boring."

Each of the 26 chapters in this book presents a general method to lead students into Scripture. Specific activities and examples illustrate how each method can be carried out across age levels from preschool to adult. You can use your common sense and experience in adapting the material in this book to your own unique class, situation, teaching style. Besides being useful in themselves, the suggestions are meant to be catalysts for your own creative ideas.

With the 26 methods described here and through the Holy Spirit working in us, we can entice our students to taste God's Word. Once their appetite is whetted, they will be more apt to turn to the Bible for daily nourishment. They might even come to devour it!

1: Read
the Bible

Two college freshmen who were bombarded with questions from Scripture by a fundamentalist on campus were made painfully aware of their ignorance. They asked me what they could do to know Scripture better. I recommended a book: the Bible itself. A simple way to get students to know the Bible is to have them read it. In your religion classes, opt for a textbook that is woven with Scripture and that sends the students to the Bible. If possible, have a Bible for each student. (Attractive, inexpensive Bibles are available through the American Bible Society, P.O. Box 5656, Grand Central Station, New York, NY 10163.)

Sharing the Light of Faith: The National Catechetical Directory recommends that older students use the Bible as a supplementary text (n. 264). Beginning readers, too, should have the joy of reading the Bible through carefully selected passages or adapted versions. Some of the following suggestions and activities might be helpful toward immersing students in the Bible:

• In class allow God's Word to speak to your students directly. Give them time to read the Bible. Take them to church or some other quiet place and have them spread out as far away from one another as possible to read, reflect, and pray over a passage. This is not wasted time. It underlines the importance you place on Bible reading.

• Prepare for upcoming scriptural readings together. Use helps like the *Share the Word* program published by the Paulist Fathers (3010 Fourth St., NE, Washington, DC 20017). Discuss the readings. Pray over them. Let students themselves conduct these weekly preparation sessions.

• Assign biblical passages as homework to be discussed in the next class. Older students can be challenged to read a short book like the Gospel of Mark in one sitting.

• Acquaint your students with the structure of the Bible and instruct them in the mechanics of finding their way around in it. Have them look at the table of contents and answer questions such as the following:

1. *What are the two main divisions of the Bible?*
2. *What are the subdivisions?*
3. *Which books are named after men? After women?*
4. *Which books seem to contain history?*
5. *Which books are in pairs?*

6. *Which books are popular?*
7. *Which books have you never heard of?*
8. *What is the first book in the Bible? The last?*
9. *What is the shortest book in the Bible? The longest?*
10. *Which one would you like to read? Why?*

• Teach scriptural references by comparing them to an address. For example:

Jeremiah	Title (City)
17:	Chapter (Street)
7-8	Verses (House Number)

• Point out how chapters and verses are marked on the pages of the Bible. Make sure the students understand where the chapters and verses begin.

• Ask questions that make use of interesting cross references and footnotes.

• To familiarize your students with the abbreviations of the books, play this "Travel" game:

First make flashcards of some Bible abbreviations. Then direct one student to stand beside the desk of a classmate. Have the two students race to name the book that corresponds to the abbreviation shown. The winner gets to stand beside the next player's desk. See who in the class can travel the farthest.

• Hold a contest in which the winner is the one who discovers the most biblical books in a word search puzzle. (See Illustration A in Appendix.)

• Have a student name a book of the Bible and call on someone to tell the books that come before and after it. The one who answers names yet another book.

• Provide practice in looking up verses and in writing scriptural references. A creative activity that makes this task fun is the following:

Distribute a letter from God composed of lines from the Bible given in the form of references. In order to read the letter, the students must look up the references and write only the words of the verse that are indicated. When they are finished, they should slowly and prayerfully read what they have written.

Here is a sample "love letter from God" based on texts from *The New American Bible* and with the answers provided:

*Dear*_____

Is 43:1 (words 24-32)	*I have called you by name: you are mine.*
Jer 31:3 (8-14)	*With age-old love I have loved you.*
Deut 1:31 (13-32)	*Your God carried you, as a parent carries a child, all along your journey until you arrived at this place.*
Is 55:10 (1-17)	*Though the mountains leave their place and the hills be shaken, my love shall never leave you.*
Jn 15:9 (1-11)	*As the Father has loved me, so I have loved you.*
Sgs 8:6 (1-8)	*Set me as a seal on your heart.*
Ps 50:15 (1-12)	*Then call upon me in time of distress; I will rescue you.*
	Love,
	God

Teach the children to read Scripture as they would a letter from someone very important in their lives, slowly wringing the meaning out of every phrase, reading between the lines, and reading certain parts over and over.

• Challenge the students to translate the following recipe for a *Bible Cake*. The answers are in parentheses.

½ lb Judges 5:25 *(butter)*
2 c Jeremiah 6:20 *(sugar)*
½ doz Jeremiah 17:11 *(eggs)*
3½ c I Kings 4:22 *(flour)*
Pinch of Leviticus 2:13 *(salt)*
2 tsp Amos 4:5 *(yeast: baking powder)*
1½ c Judges 4:19 *(milk)*

2 c Nahum 3:11 *(figs)*
2 c I Samuel 30:12 *(raisins)*
1 c Numbers 17:23 *(almonds)*
2 tsp I Samuel 14:25 *(honey)*
II Chronicles 9:9 *(spices: cinnamon, ground cloves, nutmeg)*
Then see Proverbs 23:14 *(Beat)*

Bake 1-1½ hours. Makes 2 loaves.

(Source Unknown)

• Hold a contest for finding verses as described in Chapter 21, *Play*.

• Design activities for which the students look up passages to locate information. For example, to locate the seven last words of Jesus, give them these clues: Luke 23:34, Luke 23:43, John 19:26-27, John 19:28, Mark 14:34, John 19:30, Luke 23:46.

"Jesus Carries the Cross" from *Sharing the Passion*

Or to find images that John used for Jesus, give these references: John 6:35, John 8:12, John 10:7, John 10:11, John 11:25, John 15:1.

Or have them search for any general topic such as animals, birds, colors, flowers, mothers, or fathers.

These searches can be in the form of a matching exercise. For example, have the students match the seven sorrows of Mary with the verses that describe them (as below):

1. ____John 19:25-27   A. The flight into Egypt
2. ____Luke 2:33-35   B. The prophecy of Simeon
3. ____Luke 2:41-50   C. Jesus lost in the Temple
4. ____Luke 23:47-55   D. Meeting Jesus carrying his cross
5. ____Matthew 2:13-18   E. Mary at the foot of the cross
6. ____Mark 15:16-22   F. Jesus taken down from the cross
7. ____John 19:38-42   G. The burial of Jesus

(*Answers:* 1. B, 2. C, 3. E, 4. F, 5. D, 6. G, 7. A)

• Invite students to match scriptural references with summaries of verses, or let them look up the references and summarize the verses themselves.

• Devise scriptural searches to give the students practice writing scriptural references.

For example: Hunting for proverbs that they might like;
Finding the names used for Jesus in a particular gospel;
Locating some examples of the humanness of Jesus;
Looking for the names of Christian virtues in the epistles of the New Testament.
Searching for verses on a certain theme: faith, love, prayer, forgiveness, or mercy.

• Direct independent reading of Scripture by providing guides for students to use as they read. Ask them to answer simple questions, or finish an incomplete chart, or fill in an outline, or complete a poem with words missing, such as the one based on I Samuel 16-18:16, 26. (See Illustration B in Appendix.)

All of these activities are intended to prepare students for reading of the Bible. Remind them that God is present in the words of Scripture and that God's Word is meant for them. Encourage them to expect God to speak directly to them in certain verses.

In discussing the Gospel story of the woman who was cured by touching Jesus' cloak, Louis Evely wrote in his book, *That Man Is You:*

> Now everybody'd touched Him, everybody'd hustled Him, still nobody'd been cured or transformed. Only one had touched Him with faith; and a profound sense of well-being coursed through her; she was cured. As for us, we all read the Gospels now and then. But if we approach them like an ordinary book they'll produce no extraordinary effect on us. We have to read them the way we'd have touched Christ: with the same reverence, the same faith, the same expectancy.

With this kind of guidance, our students will learn to read Scripture not merely with their minds, but with their hearts.

2: Proclaim
the Good News

It is very important that we teach our students how to proclaim Scripture. Mumbling it, racing through it, or mutilating it is not proclaiming. Once at a parish liturgy, a lector praying the Responsorial Psalm said, "May my tongue cleave to my plate *(palate)* if I forget you Jerusalem." The picture that image conjured up did nothing for the spirit of prayer!

To prepare students to proclaim the Word, talk about eye contact, enunciation, expression, projection, pronunciation, and poise.

Challenge the students to look at the listeners as much as possible. Tell them to let their eyes read ahead of their voice so that strings of words are taken in and then recited without looking at the page.

Encourage students to enunciate and to use expression. Tell them about Demosthenes, a Greek orator who practiced by filling his mouth with marbles and then trying to speak clearly. Have the students exaggerate as they practice, so that even if stage fright overcomes them, their reading will still be better than before they practiced.

To ensure that they are heard, have the students concentrate on projecting their voices to the person in the farthest corner of the room. Let them practice with a microphone and try adjusting it for themselves. Build their courage by having them repeat words they stumble over. For real sticklers, direct them to books like *Lector's Guide to Biblical Pronunciation* by Joseph M. Staudacher (Our Sunday Visitor).

Tactfully call attention to those nervous habits that students tend to develop when facing a group: twisting a strand of hair, playing with a button, shaking a leg, clearing their throats, or anything else that will distract from the Word.

Tape record the students or even videotape them if possible. Then have them evaluate themselves and one another. Provide opportunities in class for students to proclaim the Word (See Chapter 25, *Celebrate.*) Most of all, be a model for your students by proclaiming any scriptural passage your lesson calls for with reverence, power, and clarity.

3:   Tell
the Bible Stories

A delightful way to teach Scripture is actually to tell biblical stories. This is, after all, the way Scripture was first handed down. Adults as well as children can be fascinated by the stories in the Bible.

The vocabulary and the content of stories should be adapted to the audience. Children do not need to hear all the details, but they do enjoy updated versions of the stories they've grown up with. For example, in telling the story of the multiplication of the loaves and fish, remark that the nearest fast-food restaurant was a mile away.

Flesh out the stories in the Bible when only the skeleton is given. You can do research or use your imagination and common sense to fill in the details. Consult commentaries like the *Jerome Biblical Commentary* for background information. Imagine yourself in the situations described and notice the surroundings and the expressions on people's faces. Put yourself in the shoes of the main characters and sense their feelings and reactions. Ask questions about what happens.

In preparing to tell the story of the daughter of Jairus, for example, visualize the crowd at the lakeside and Jairus elbowing his way up to Jesus and then falling at his feet. Feel Jairus' relief as Jesus agrees to go with him, his frustration when Jesus stops to speak to the woman who touched his cloak, and Jairus' despair when he is told that his daughter has died.

Ask yourself: What did Jesus see and hear when he entered Jairus' house? What did the mourners say when they made fun of him? How did he feel as he put them out?

Imagine what the little girl experienced coming back to consciousness and feeling someone holding her hand. Think what it was like for her to open her eyes and see Jesus looking down at her. How did her parents react? What happened after Jesus said, "Give her something to eat" (Mark 5:21-43)?

A story is more effective if you insert dramatic pauses and gestures, but the success of your presentation is largely determined by your voice: its quality, its pace, and its expression. Before venturing to tell a story, practice until you are very familiar with it. Tell it in front of a mirror or before an honest friend. Tape record your story for a real revelation about your storytelling techniques.

For young children, telling stories through a puppet adds variety and charm. The puppet can be purchased or made out of a sock, a mitten, a popsicle stick, or a balloon. A favorite story becomes even more engrossing the second or third time around if the children are invited to add key lines, gestures, and sound effects.

Children of all ages like chalk talk stories. These are stories accompanied by simple stick figures and line drawings done with chalk. (Use colored chalk, if possible.) You do not have to be a Picasso to do this. In fact, if your art is worse than the students' art, they enjoy it all the more. (See Illustration C in Appendix for pictures you can draw as you tell the parable of the Prodigal Son.)

Encourage the students to tell biblical stories to other children: younger brothers and sisters, children they babysit, or children at a day-care center. You might arrange to have your students tell stories to small groups of younger students in another class. You'll be surprised to see how well they imitate you.

The Crosiers/Gene Plaisted

4: Dramatize the Scripture Stories

If you want to wake up your students, act out a story from the Bible. To teach the story of the burning bush, dress like Moses, bearded and with staff in hand, and, believe me, you'll have everyone's attention. To demonstrate Peter's Pentecost sermon, one second-grade teacher jumped up on a reading chair and shouted, "Jesus is risen. He's alive!" Then she jumped down again to become a member of the crowd wondering, "What's the matter with them? Are they drunk?" She was very effective.

An alternative to acting out the story yourself is having the students enact it. Children remember best those classes in which they were actively involved. What religion classes from your childhood do you recall best? Probably the ones in which you played a part. One day in checking my English students' journals, I found that Barbara had written that the most exciting thing that happened to her that day was being asked to come to the front of the class to demonstrate the word "saunter." Most students love to act. Some are born hams. The introverts prefer to act out stories using puppets or paper cutouts on the overhead. One shy girl in my class, though, played the apple tree in the Garden of Eden. She just stood there dangling the apple from her fingers, and she stole the show.

Many episodes from both the Old and New Testaments beg to be enacted—from Genesis (Abraham and the visitors, Jacob and Esau, Rebekah, Joseph) to Acts of the Apostles (the death of Stephen, the conversion of Paul, Peter's escape from prison and the journeys of Paul and Barnabas). Let the children act out the miracles and parables from the gospels. Even the youngest, who can't read or write, can mime a story, put on a shadow play, or stand in place as part of a "living picture" production. Sometimes the entire class can provide actions for a story simultaneously. For example, children love to pretend to be seeds in the Parable of the Seed. They are especially good at being the seeds that are choked to death.

Let older students interview the queen of Sheba, or the blind man healed by Jesus, the apostle John, or Lazarus after he was raised from the dead. Have them produce a talk show with Noah and God, or with Saul, David, and Solomon. Help them plan a TV tribute to Joshua who led the Hebrews into the promised land, or the boy who handed over his loaves and fish, or Joseph of Arimathea who gave his tomb for Jesus' burial. They can stage a courtroom scene where witnesses declare Jesus is alive based on the post-Resurrection stories. Let them prepare commercials or 60-second radio spots with a prophetic message or a piece of "Good News."

Have them write and present a play about Esther and invite the audience to applaud the heroes and hiss the villains (or use noisemakers to show their dislike) as the Jewish people do when the Esther story is part of their celebration of Purim. Encourage the students to use costumes and props and to draw scenery on the blackboard. (See Illustration D in Appendix for a play about Esther.)

"Esther Before Xerxes" from *Women of Israel*

For variety in dramatizing the Bible, use choral reading. Have groups of students each recite a Beatitude, or direct small groups to chime in during the recitation of Psalm 150 for a cumulative effect. Rewrite a passage in Scripture so that the story is told by characters alternating with a chorus. Include directions for the voices like *strong, soft, echoing,* or *gruff.* (See Illustration E for a sample choral reading about Abraham that reinforces his importance as the first patriarch.)

Children can experience the psalms as liturgy by praying them in different ways. Divide the class into two sides and have them alternate praying sections of a psalm. Psalms that are easily prayed with students this way are Psalms 1, 4, 19, 33, 56, 63, 86, 92, 112, and 139. Another way to pray the psalms is to have a reader pray it with the class repeating an antiphon after each verse or section. Psalms and suggested antiphons for this method are:

Psalm 16, I trust in you, O Lord.
Psalm 29, Praise the Lord.
Psalm 91, You are my defender.
Psalm 96, The Lord is king.
Psalm 100, Alleluia, alleluia
Psalm 138, I thank you, Lord.
Psalm 147, Sing praise to our God.

5: Relate
Scripture to the World

By relating the Bible to contemporary situations, we help our students to conclude that it is grounded in reality, that it mirrors common human experiences, and that it has a message for us now. Have the students comb the newspapers for modern-day characters and events that are similar to ones in the Bible. Encourage them to find a modern-day Job, Judas, or Paul, and perhaps a new Exodus, Exile, or crucifixion. When teaching the gospels, have the students ask people what Jesus means to them today, or ask the students to give concrete examples of people they know who live the Beatitudes.

"Eve Is Tempted" from *Stories from the Old Testament*

Relate the people in the Bible to the children and their own lives. Let them see that Adam and Eve progressed through the same stages of sin that they do: being attracted to it, questioning the commandment, entertaining the idea, yielding to temptation, being ashamed, and then being alienated from God. Point out that just as Abraham was called to a journey of faith, so are they. Show how the beautiful friendship between David and Jonathan can be a model for their own relationships. Help them to identify with impetuous Peter, who was brash and disloyal, but who also loved Jesus.

Plan experiences for the students that link their lives to the lives of biblical characters. For example, when teaching about Hosea and his unfaithful wife Gomer, lead students in a discussion about family and the ingredients of true love. Ask them to write a letter in Hosea's name to Ann Landers, or invite them to compose a love poem, as Hosea might have written it.

To further personalize the Bible, have the students read certain verses and give an example of what they mean for someone their age. Read psalms to them and ask them to suggest appropriate times when these might be used for prayer. Suggest that they try to answer the questions that Jesus asked people in the gospels:

> What do you want me to do for you? (Matthew 20:32)
> And you, who do you say that I am? (Matthew 16:15)
> Whoever lives and believes in me will never die. Do you believe this? (John 11:26 JB).
> Have I been with you all this time, _____(Name)_____, and you still do not know me? (John 14:9 JB).

Have the students bring in their family Bible, show it, and talk about how their family uses it.

To introduce literary forms of the Bible, draw parallels with things familiar to the students. For example: The Proverbs are like bumper stickers, buttons, or posters. The Song of Songs is like a love-song. The epistles are like letters we receive today from the bishop. The parables Jesus told are like Aesop's fables.

When the opportunity arises, relate aspects of the Jewish faith in the Bible to the practices of Jewish people today: the celebration of feastdays like Passover (the Exodus), Hanukkah (the rededication of the Temple by Judas Maccabeus), and Purim (liberation through Esther); the Sabbath; the shema (Deuteronomy 6:4-5) which is prayed every day; and dietary laws. Invite a rabbi or a Jewish person to speak to the students about the Hebrew Scriptures. You might even plan a field trip to a synagogue.

One project that could involve the whole family is to have the students compile a photo album and then use verses from the Book of Psalms as captions. Through efforts like these, your students will gradually come to interpret their lives and their world through God's Word.

6: Correlate Scripture with the Arts

It's essential that you try to correlate Scripture with other subjects. For example, supplement your lessons with literature. Many catechists have discovered the power of *The Velveteen Rabbit* by Margery Williams, or *The Giving Tree* by Shel Silverstein to supplement a lesson. For guidance in finding appropriate books, refer to publications like *Children's Literature for Religious Education* by Robert J. Fitzsimmons (Peter Li, Inc.) and *Trailing Clouds of Glory* by Madeleine L'Engle (The Westminster Press). Reading from a book for five minutes at the beginning of each class serves to settle the children. Even high school students will anticipate these five minutes if the book is well chosen.

In addition to children's books and adolescent literature, poetry, plays, and short stories also echo biblical themes. James Weldon Johnson's poem "The Creation" is a strong and moving interpretation of the Genesis story. The short story "The Gift of the Magi" by O. Henry is a beautiful expression of the Christmas themes of love and sacrifice. Archibald MacLeish's play *J.B.* can give older students insights into the story of Job.

Introduce music into your scriptural lessons: classical and popular, religious and secular. Analyze popular songs to see whether they contradict or support gospel values. Play classical pieces while the children do independent or group work as a stimulus or background for prayer, or as an approach to a lesson. Make use of old spirituals like "Amazing Grace" and also contemporary Christian songs. Christmas carols contain enough theology to teach the facts and the meaning of the infancy narratives, while Handel's "Messiah" is a glorious prelude to a lesson on Easter.

"The Annunciation" from *Mary and the Rosary*

Use art masterpieces. Tell the story of Mary's life or the last days of Jesus through slides of famous paintings. Take a field trip to an art museum to see paintings depicting biblical events or visit the history museum to find artifacts from biblical times.

Older students will enjoy learning the rudiments of calligraphy so that they can letter Scripture verses in the manner of the early manuscripts. Have them use calligraphy pens. Penpoints from the C series work well. India ink is the best medium, but watercolor paint applied to the points with a brush can be substituted. Another alternative is to use felt-tipped pens with points shaped for lettering. Instruct the students to keep their paper straight in front of them and to hold the pens at a forty-five degree angle at all times. Suggest that they hold their breath while making long, straight strokes. Give them a model sheet of the alphabet. (See Illustration F in Appendix.)

7: Share
Personal Impact of Scripture

Faith is contagious. As a believing Christian, you have more impact on your students than any textbook series or audiovisual could ever have. It's no surprise then that a key technique in teaching Scripture is personal sharing. Be willing to share what the Bible means to you. Tell about a time that you discovered something new in a passage, or a time when verses had a specific meaning for you. In Jeremiah 23:29, God asks, "Is not my word like fire. . .like a hammer shattering rocks?" Ask students if a scriptural passage has ever been like lightning streaking through them, or like a hammer that God hits them over the head with.

Saint Augustine let us know that his conversion was attributed to Scripture. As he sat under a tree, he heard a child's voice repeating, "Take and read." He opened the Bible and God overtook him. Francis of Assisi shared his experience of Scripture with his brothers. Tradition says that when he opened the Bible at random three times, the verses he found became the foundation for the Franciscan community. More recently, the singer and composer John Michael Talbot used the same process to come to a decision during a crisis point in his life. The story is related in his biography *Troubadour for the Lord* by Dan O'Neill (Crossroads Publishing Company).

Your sharing can be integrated into teacher-student interaction during the development of a lesson, or it can be part of a celebration or prayer service. It can even take the form of comments on the papers of individual students.

I'd like to share here one of my personal experiences with God's Word. I entered the convent in the sixties, a time of great upheaval. The very year I entered, the Sisters I had idolized began leaving left and right. I began to wonder if I should leave, too. One day I was alone in chapel with desperate thoughts running through my mind like, "What am I doing here? Religious life is falling apart. Help, Lord! What am I supposed to do?"

Since no one was around, I walked up to the Bible enthroned in front of chapel. I looked down at the page, and the words of Matthew 19:29 JB leaped out at me: "And everyone who has left houses, brothers, sisters, father, mother, children, or land for the sake of my name will be repaid a hundred times over and also inherit eternal life." I stayed. Some may call it coincidence, but for me that day, God spoke.

David S. Strickler

Invariably your sharing of personal stories, like this one of mine, will spark student sharing. And everyone will leave class with a stronger faith, maybe you more than anyone else, after hearing your students' experiences.

19

8: Rewrite
Scripture Prayers

One way to give students insight into Scripture is to have them rewrite it. For example, suggest that they put the Prodigal Son story in a twentieth century setting. The Good Samaritan parable is easier to identify with if you relate it to a driver stranded on the highway who is ignored by people whose bumper stickers read: "Honk if you love Jesus."

The psalms, too, lend themselves to rewriting. For example, here is Psalm 23, the Good Shepherd psalm, as rewritten by a student:

> God is my world. With him I don't need anything.
> He helps me to be calm. He keeps me out of trouble.
> He makes me live.
> He keeps me cool for him.
> Even though it's dark around me, he makes me unafraid.
> Bad things don't scare me because he is with me.
> His hands keep everything all right.
> He has my life mapped out.
> He makes me brave in front of people who hate me.
> He blesses me. My joy explodes.

Besides parables and psalms, students can write their own commandments, proverbs, beatitudes, and accounts of creation. Passages that lend

"Noah Trusted in God" from *Stories from the Old Testament*

themselves especially well to paraphrase are Proverbs 31:10-31 (the ideal wife), Habakkuk 3:17-19 (having faith in times of trouble), Luke 1:46-55 (the Magnificat), and I Corinthians 13 (the hymn to charity).

Students might also supply "unwritten chapters" of Scripture, for example, Adam's and Eve's reactions to the murder of Abel, Noah's explanation of the ark, episodes from the hidden life of Jesus, and Mary's life after Pentecost.

Bible stories can be recast in the form of plays or poems. They can be retold in a particular dialect: southern, western or Black. (See Illustration G in Appendix for a sample "recast" Bible story called "Genesis According to Room 21.")

9: Research Biblical Topics

Recommend to your students books and articles that throw light on Scripture. For example, *God's Smuggler* by Brother Andrew, and *Hiding Place* by Corrie ten Boom. Introduce them to these magazines: *The Bible Today* (Liturgical Press), *Share the Word* (Paulist Press), *God's Word Today* (Box 7705, Ann Arbor, Michigan 48107), and *Biblical Archaeology Review*.

Develop in them the habit of independent study. Students *and* catechists can always learn more about the Bible. Recently I read that after Noah went into the ark, Yahweh closed the door behind him. I had never noticed that detail in the Bible story. I looked it up and there it was: "And Yahweh closed the door behind Noah."

I thought I knew Psalm 23 until I read the book *A Shepherd Looks at Psalm 23* by Phillip Keller (Zondervan). The phrase "He restoreth my soul" is so much more meaningful now since I've learned about "cast sheep." A cast sheep is a sheep that has turned over on its back and can't get up again. It struggles frantically and is vulnerable to attack. In this position, gases build up in the rumen of the sheep and cut off circulation to the extremities. In the summer a sheep can die in a few hours. If it's cool, the agony can last for several days.

"Abraham Tends His Sheep" from *Stories from the Old Testament*

A good shepherd is always on the watch for cast sheep. When he finds one, he rolls it over on its side and lifts it onto its feet. Then he straddles it and holds it upright, rubbing its limbs to restore circulation, all the while speaking to it encouragingly. It takes a long time to restore a cast down sheep. This concept deepened my appreciation of the good shepherd who "restoreth my soul."

Assign reports on the Bible. Some possible topics:

The process of the composition of the Bible
Deuterocanonical books
Apocryphal books
Translations of the Bible
Versions like the Thumb Bible, the Vinegar Bible, the
    Wicked Bible, and the Devil's Bible
The peoples of the Bible
The Israelites
Life in biblical times: customs, food, clothing, shelter, coins,
    measurements of time
Palestine
Archeological finds like the Dead Sea Scrolls
Jewish feasts
The evangelists: their audiences, styles, and symbols
The Hebrew alphabet
Number symbolism in the Bible

Help your students read maps that show biblical territories and trace various journeys. Acquaint them with handbooks of the Bible, dictionaries of the Bible, and concordances.

Invite students to ask people they know what their favorite book of the Bible is or their favorite biblical story. Have them search for the role of the Bible in the lives of famous men and women.

More advanced students can read the *Constitution on Divine Revelation*, whole or in part, and do a report on their findings. (See Illustration H in Appendix for a study guide that can be used with this Constitution. It is based on the collection of documents edited by Austin Flannery, O.P. (Costello Publishing Company).

10: Create Scriptural Arts

If it's true that we remember twenty percent of what we hear and ninety percent of what we do, then time spent in creative activity is time well spent. Let the students translate the Word of Scripture into art, sometimes working in groups to foster community. Plan for them to experience different media—from fingerpaint to crayons on sandpaper. For a simple and clean art activity, let the children draw on the blackboard with water. For an outside activity, sidewalk art done with chalk brings joy to artists and observers alike.

Scriptural verses can be lettered on posters, buttons, banners, balloons, mobiles, bumper stickers, bookmarks, placemats, holy cards, pennants, seashells, driftwood, doorknob hangers, all-occasion greeting cards, T-shirts, paperweights made from rocks, and wooden plaques coated with shellac. To heighten the interest of older students in these projects, teach calligraphy. (See Chapter 6, *Correlate.*)

Students can use their ingenuity to design book jackets, record album covers, posters, bulletin boards, banners, billboards, and even commemorative stamps based on a biblical book or theme. They can fill a display case with an exhibit on the prophets or on the parables. Banners can be hung in the school hall or the church. Each child can hang a personal banner from the front of his or her desk.

Biblical stories can be illustrated in many ways. Children can make huge murals of creation, Jesus' miracles, or his last days. They can make tiny pictures out of their fingerprints, using colored ink pads and filling in details with felt-tipped pens. They can present a story in the form of a torn-paper picture, a yarn and cloth picture, a tryptich (a three-paneled picture), a cartoon, a collage of magazine pictures, a comic book, or a children's storybook. Freehand drawings from all the children can be compiled into one class booklet. This can be the conventional bound booklet (stapled or tied with yarn) or the accordian type. Laminate the best drawings and use them to tell biblical stories in the future. The young artists will be proud when you ask to keep their work, and other classes will be delighted to see children's art while they listen to a story.

People of the Bible become unforgettable when children reflect on them and their lives in an attempt to represent them. They can design a coat of arms for Abraham, Gideon, Peter, or Paul. They can cut silhouettes of various people in a story or make puppets out of paper bags, paper plates, socks, clothespins, or simply by pasting paper figures on the end of a pencil. Children who are artistic might enjoy making a portfolio of biblical portraits using pen and ink, watercolor, or pastels. Brief character descriptions can accompany portraits of the patriarchs, heroines of the Bible, or the apostles.

Art projects for the more ambitious catechist and students can be planned in class and then carried out at home. Abraham's sacrifice of Isaac or the Annunciation can be portrayed in wire sculpture, aluminum foil, or papier-mache. Dioramas made with shoe boxes are suited to scenes with more than two characters: the Stations of the Cross, or colorful stories like Daniel in the lions' den, or Peter walking on the water. Scenery is crayoned or painted on the inside of the box, and figures and props are made to stand by means of pipe cleaners or tabs glued to the bottom of the box.

Mobiles with symbols related to a biblical book or theme create a joyful atmosphere in a classroom. These .can be made from multidimensional figures decorated with drawn pictures, magazine pictures, or construction-paper symbols and suspended from a hanger. Experiment with different shapes, sizes, and colors.

Stained-glass windows can be designed simply by drawing a picture on paper and lacing it with thick black lines. For a more realistic effect, paste tissue paper on strips of black construction paper. A group of students can transform an entire bulletin board into a stained-glass window of the Good Shepherd, the Passion, or a patron saint.

Mosaic, a form of religious art popular in the fourth century, can be created using large or small pieces of construction paper or colored sections of magazine pages. For different effects, students can use paper punch holes (picked up and placed with a straight pin), Easter egg shells, or a mixture of seeds, beans, noodles, and rice.

Students can construct models of the Ark of the Covenant, Solomon's Temple, or the Holy Land. They can shape symbols that represent Moses, David, or Mary from clay. Or, make them from this simple bread dough: Thoroughly mix

> 4 cups flour,
> 1 cup salt,
> 1½ cups water.
> After the children have molded their
> symbols, bake at 350° until hardened.
> (Large pieces may take up to an hour.)

Photo essays made with magazine pictures or students' own photographs are something they will want to keep. One of the psalms or Jesus' Sermon on the Mount would make good subjects. Students can also put together mock photo albums of a particular family in the Bible, for example, Abraham's family or the family of King David. They can draw original illustrations and write captions for each "photo."

Boxes can be decorated on each side according to a theme: a glory box, an Easter box, a joy box, a box on the Works of Mercy. Or you may wish to have younger children make a religion box to hold all their art projects at home. Their parents might appreciate this.

During Advent a small Christmas tree can become a Jesse tree, containing symbols of the people and events associated with the Messiah. The tree takes its name from Isaiah 11:1, "Thus saith the Lord God: There shall come forth a rod out of the root of Jesse, and a flower shall rise up out of his root." Jesse was the father of King David. The students can create the symbols from paper or from other materials and objects. (See Illustrations I & J in Appendix for some sample Jesse tree symbols and a Jesse Tree.)

A parallel Advent activity is the more recent custom of making a Chrismon tree (Christmas + monogram). The Chrismon tree bears symbols of Jesus from the New Testament. While the children hang their symbols, related scriptural texts might be read. Possible figures for the Chrismon tree are Mary, Joseph, the star, manger, shepherd, angel, sheep, three kings, gifts, fish, dove, grapes, wheat, vine, crown, rock, alpha and omega symbols, Chi-Rho, anchor, and cross.

When you have children doing creative activities, keep in mind that the end product is not as important as the process!

11: Add Humor to Scripture Study

Jesus vindicates laughter. His death and resurrection give us reason to face today and tomorrow with joy. Our church, therefore, has the potential to be a laughing church. In *The Little Prince* by Antoine de Saint Exupery, the Little Prince leaves his friend the gift of laughter. We can give our children the gift of laughter, too. Joy, one of the fruits of the Holy Spirit, should mark our teaching of the Good News.

As we read Scripture we should be attuned to the divine sense of humor. Alert your students to the fun in the Noah story with its animal parade (play Bill Cosby's recorded version). Children will enjoy knowing that the Jonah story has a man-eating whale and a plant-eating worm. Recall for them, too, the humor in the predicament of Peter as he slips into the sea after walking on the water. The story about Jesus arranging for tax money to appear in the mouth of a fish is as much a practical joke as a miracle. Also, when Jesus says that it is as difficult for a rich man to get into heaven as for a camel to go through the eye of a needle, the comparison is preposterous and funny, especially if the camel is Bactrian (two-humped)!

The humor continues through Acts. Rhoda is so excited to see Peter at the door that she runs to tell everyone of his arrival and forgets to let him in. And then there is Eutychus who dozes during one of Paul's ser-

"Eutyches Falls from the Window" from *Witnessing Jesus in the Early Church*

mons and falls out of the window. We can laugh at that because, luckily, Paul was able to bring him back to life.

Good speakers know the secret of sprinkling their talks with jokes and funny anecdotes to keep their audience with them. Catechists can employ this secret to sustain interest and to create a happy atmosphere. In the Bible itself we find the words "A joyful heart is the health of the body, but a depressed spirit dries up the bones" (Proverbs 17:22).

It's a good idea to jot down jokes related to Scripture when you read or hear them. Here is a start for your collection:

ADAM AND EVE—One day Adam and Eve and their two boys were walking past the gates of Paradise, which was guarded by the cherubim. Abel inquired, "What's that, Dad?" Adam replied, "That's where we used to live before your mother ate us out of house and home."

LOT'S WIFE—A teacher was telling the story of the flight of Lot's family from Sodom. When she got to the part where Lot's wife looked back and turned into a pillar of salt, one child remarked, "That's nothing. Once my mother looked back and turned into a telephone pole."

EXODUS/BIBLICAL TRUTH—When Jimmy came home from religion class, his mother asked, "What did you learn today, Jimmy?" He said, "God sent Moses to rescue the Israelites. When they came to the Red Sea, Moses had engineers build a pontoon bridge. As the Israelites crossed they saw the Egyptian tanks coming. So Moses radioed headquarters to send bombers…" "Jimmy," interrupted his mother, "Is that really what your teacher said?" "Well, not exactly," he replied. "But if I told it her way, you'd never believe it."

GOSPEL STORIES—When Jesus exorcized the possessed man and sent the devils into the pigs, that was the first recorded instance of deviled ham.

Reviewing the role of the "other son" in the story of the Prodigal Son, the teacher said, "There was someone who was not happy at the thought of the feast and who had no desire to go to it. Who was this?" A small voice piped up, "The fatted calf."

12: Sing Scripture-Based Songs

When we teach children to sing biblical songs, snatches will come back to them for the rest of their lives. Not only is singing "praying twice," but it has the power to create an *esprit de corps* among the children. It's a real community experience, especially if the song involves harmony. Songs can be used as prayers to open the class. They can be inserted in the course of a lesson for a change of pace. They also make a good vehicle for the children's response of gratitude and praise at the close of a class. If your voice sounds like a cat with its tail caught in the door, use records or tapes, but let the children sing.

Find musical arrangements of Scripture and teach them. The psalms are song-prayers. They are meant to be sung. Refer to books like *The Psalm Locator: Where to Find Songs Based on the Psalter*, edited by Anthony Lawrence (Resource Publications). Many contemporary Christian albums contain songs with lyrics that are either direct words of Scripture or based on Scripture. Many of these have catchy melodies that bring the gospel stories to life and present God's message in a lucid and memorable way. Such albums are available at Christian book stores.

Encourage even those students who are not blessed with angelic voices. You might tell them what Thomas a Kempis said: "If you cannot sing like the nightingale and the lark, then sing like the crows and frogs, who sing as God meant them to."

"The Exodus" from *Stories from the Old Testament*

We can do music ministers a service by teaching songs for liturgy. You might consult your music minister to find out the songs he or she would like to add to the school or parish repertoire.

Little children love to sing songs with gestures. Make them up, or let them make them up. High school students can be challenged to write original scriptural songs. They can write ballads about biblical personages or events, e.g., The Ballad of Joseph, Son of Jacob; the Ballad of the Great Escape (Exodus); the Ballad of Mary Magdalen. They can set the psalms to music or compose meditation songs on the sayings of Jesus. They can write parodies and sing them, such as the following:

Samson (To the chorus of "Yankee Doodle")

Samson, mighty champion,
Samson, with your long hair
You can beat the Philistines,
But of their women beware.

Mustard Seed (To "Twinkle, Twinkle Little Star")

Tiny, tiny mustard seed,
You are small but great indeed.
You will be the largest tree.
Many nests in you we'll see.
Tiny, tiny mustard seed,
You are small but great indeed.

Those students who play musical instruments can be invited to accompany the singing in class celebrations or parish liturgies. In this way they will form the habit of sharing their gifts with the community.

13: Dance in Response to Scripture

Choreograph scriptural verses so that the children are able to involve their whole bodies in response to God's Word. Devise steps for some scriptural-based songs. Play music and let the children invent their own dances. They might do one called "I Love Creation," or "The Dance of the Healed Lepers," or another called "Rejoicing over the Lost Sheep." To allow for more freedom of movement, hold the class in the gym or outside.

Older students are good at working out liturgical movements for songs. In particular, those students who have had dancing lessons can be called upon to do an interpretive dance of a biblical passage. For wider participation, students can add rhythm instruments, tambourines, drums, or simply clap their hands to the music. (See Illustration K in Appendix for sample dance movements to accompany the Our Father.)

Akin to dancing is cheerleading. Let groups of cheerleaders work out routines that correspond to events in the Bible, e.g., a pyramid formation in a mime interpretation of the tower of Babel, a chant with motions for the battle of Jericho, or a cheer about the Beatitudes.

Children dancing can provide high-level entertainment for a school celebration or program. In addition it can enhance a First Communion Mass, a scriptural reading, or a psalm response. Dancing is in line with biblical tradition: Miriam, Moses' sister, danced after the Israelites safely passed through the Red Sea, and David danced before the Ark of the Covenant. At the wedding feast of Cana, Jesus and Mary probably danced with their relatives and friends.

14: Memorize
to Master the Material

Once at a eucharistic celebration, I heard a reader proclaim the entire First Reading by heart. It was very striking. With a little prodding, our students are capable of similar feats.

Wary of the pitfalls of the Baltimore Catechism era, modern catechists might be reluctant to have their students memorize anything. But Pope John Paul II pointed out in *Catechesis in Our Time* that "The blossoms. . .of faith and piety do not grow in the desert places of a memoryless catechesis"(55). It is good for children to memorize Scripture, especially key verses, Jesus' words, psalms, and other prayers. In the process of memorizing a passage, they often arrive at a deeper understanding of it. Moreover, as with songs, biblical verses once memorized that run through our minds can lead us into prayer. It is good to provide our students with a rich supply of such verses.

Actually, many children enjoy memorizing. It gives them a feeling of accomplishment to be able to rattle off the names of the 12 apostles and the fruits of the Holy Spirit (Galatians 5:22-23), or to recite the Beatitudes (Matthew 5:3-10).

There are several ways to encourage the memorization of Scripture:

• Post charts marking the progress of each student.

• Display a box with verses to be drawn out and memorized.

• Every week write a verse to be memorized on the board or letter it and display it on the bulletin board.

• Write scriptural quotations on long cards. Cut them in half and distribute the halves to students. When the first half is read, the student holding the rest of the quotation stands and reads it. For a greater challenge, have the endings read first.

Teach memory devices to aid in studying Scripture. For example try this jingle to remember the order of the first 14 New Testament letters (epistles), using the first syllables of each book:
RO-CO-CO,
GAL-EPH-PHI (rhymes with "eye"),
COL-THESS-THESS,
TIM-TIM-TI,
PHIL-HEB.

Long lists are committed to memory more quickly if they are thought of in categories. For example, the books of the Old Testament are more manageable considered as the Pentateuch, historical books, wisdom books, and prophetic books. Find helpful associations. I always had trouble remembering who was the murderer and who was the victim in the first homicide until I linked Cain with "cane," a potential weapon.

Invent acronyms. To teach the three main regions of Palestine in order—Galilee, Samaria, and Judea—make a phrase or sentence with the first letters of each: G, S, J. "Good Saint Joseph" and "God sent Jesus" are possibilities. Likewise, the names and sequence of the books in the Pentateuch (Genesis, Exodus, Leviticus, Numbers, Deuteronomy) can be recalled by nonsense sentences such as this one: *Goats eat leaves, not dirt.* Or the more helpful code: Jenny has extra levis no. doubt (pronounced "deut"). The sillier the device, the easier it is to remember.

15: Discuss
Scripture for Insights

Usually discussion is more fruitful than a monologue. Some principles to keep in mind for discussion are the following:

• State the question or problem clearly and make sure students understand it and know what they are to do.

• Prepare students so that they have the information and the skills needed to carry on an intelligent discussion of the topic.

• Encourage everyone to participate and discourage anyone from monopolizing the discussion.

• Guide the students to practice courtesy by listening to one another, by expressing themselves politely, and by respecting the opinions of others.

• Keep the students on the topic.

• Summarize the discussion at the end.

Questions for discussion should be chosen carefully. Agree-disagree discussions and debates should not be such that the class arrives at a conclusion that contradicts church teachings. Questions should focus on significant ideas and have meaning for the students. They should be thought-provoking. "Why" questions are more intriguing than who, what, when, and where questions.

Discussions often reveal misconceptions. The catechist should be alert to these and correct them, if not that day, then later.

Many forms of classroom discussion can be adapted to biblical study:

• Discussion can be stimulated by means of a *continuum activity*. Ask the students a question or give them a statement and let them determine where on a continuum their response would lie. For example:

God does not answer prayers today the way they were answered in the Bible.

STRONGLY AGREE   AGREE   DISAGREE   STRONGLY DISAGREE

Responses can be marked on paper. For more concrete involvement, the students can place themselves on an imaginary line stretching across the classroom with its ends representing opposing points of view. After the discussion, students can place themselves on the line again to see which way the class has been swayed.

• A *Phillips 66 discussion* makes a good lead into a lesson. Arrange the students into groups of six. Allow them six minutes to discuss a question such as, "If you were alive when Jesus was and had seen and heard him, what would you think of him?"

• Involve the entire class in an *open discussion* of questions. To save time and to increase confidence, have students prepare the questions ahead of time. Here are sample questions to evoke reflection on the Book of Ruth: Why is Ruth a model of faithful love? What other virtues did she possess? What evidence is there that Boaz was worthy of Ruth? How was Ruth rewarded for her faithfulness? What is God showing his people by the fact that Ruth was a Moabite and not Jewish? What people today would particularly profit from reading this book?

• The same type of questions that can be discussed in a large group can be discussed in *small groups* of five, each with its own chairperson. This allows more students to participate actively. Each chairperson gives a group report. Open class discussion follows.

• Also with small groups, have an *agree-disagree discussion.* Compose a set of controversial statements like the following:

Jesus was more divine than human.

The early Christian community as described in Acts was not like the church today.

The stories in the Hebrew Scriptures have little meaning for us.

David was a greater Hebrew hero than Moses.

Divide the class into groups of five with a chairperson for each group. Direct the groups to try to come to a definite decision for each statement. Everyone should be encouraged to contribute facts, experiences, and reflective thinking for the consideration of the group. The decision of the majority in each group should be recorded. At the end of the discussion period, allow time for individuals to write summaries. In a forum, compare the results of all the groups and invite comments from the class.

• Choose a topic that lends itself to *debate* such as those suggested for the agree-disagree discussions. Let two teams debate the issue before the class. The debate begins with each side presenting its point of view in a two-minute talk. Then the participants debate. The class can vote at the end to determine which side won.

• A form of discussion called *kineposium* provides for maximum interaction among students. Its purpose is to generate and share ideas, not to debate. The topics chosen for the kineposium should allow for a diversity of opinions, for example:

How is the faith God calls us to in Scripture best shown in our lives?

Which woman in the Hebrew Scriptures most clearly prefigures Mary?

Outside of the Resurrection what do you think was Christ's most significant miracle?

Someone once said that Christianity has not failed, it's just never been tried. Which teaching of Christ seems most difficult for people to "try" today?

What message from the prophets do we most need today?

Appoint the number of secretaries needed, one for each group. The other students each receive a card listing the group numbers in different orders. (See Illustration L in Appendix.) At the signal, all go to the first group listed on their cards. After the designated time spent discussing the assigned question, a signal is again given. Everyone then moves to the next group where the secretary checks to make sure everyone is in the right group. (Secretaries do not rotate.) This process is repeated until everyone has been to each group. The secretaries then report. This is followed by a kineposium forum in which anyone may raise questions or make additions.

16: Write
on the Word of God

Creative writing assignments can lead students to delve deeper into the meaning of Scripture and help them to remember it. As students read Scripture, they can record in journals what certain verses mean to them. They can also reply to passages in the form of personal prayers to God written in their journals. More advanced students might write an entire meditation on a scriptural passage.

Have the students write a dialogue between characters, for example, between Samson and his mother after he has been blinded, or between Ezra and Nehemiah as they plan the restoration of Jerusalem, or between Thomas and John as they discuss how Jesus calmed the storm.

Invite the students to write a biblical story from a particular point of view, for example, the sacrifice of Isaac through the eyes of Isaac himself, or Bartimaeus' account of his own cure. Or they can write a story as the "other side" saw it: Satan's report of the Fall, the Egyptian view of the Exodus, the Canaanite account of the Israelite invasion, and Pilate's version of Jesus' trial.

Other writings activities that enable the students to put themselves in the shoes of people in the Bible include the following:

- logs of the Exodus, Jesus' travels, and Paul's missionary journeys

"Paul Brings Good News" from *Witnessing Jesus in the Early Church*

• diary entries of Judas Maccabeus or one of the apostles during Holy Week

• prayers that a person in the Bible like Adam, Joseph, Moses, Mary Magdalen, or Dorcas might have prayed

• letters to Adam, Judith, Thomas, or between Jacob and Uncle Laban, Mary and her cousin Elizabeth, from great-great-grandmother Eve to us, or from Jesus to us

• speeches that Moses, Isaiah, or Paul might have delivered

• a eulogy for Judith, Samuel, Lazarus, or the Good Thief

• a litany of John the Baptist or of Saint Peter

Writing activities that call for summaries of main ideas include these:

• storyboards for a television show about a biblical event

• a newscast on the battle of Jericho or the Sermon on the Mount

• a telegram describing one of Jesus' miracles in 15 words or less

• headlines summarizing major happenings in the life of Jesus

• titles for biographies of people in the Bible, for example, Saul's biography might be called *Heart of Darkness*, David's *The Loved One*, and Solomon's *The Power and the Glory*.

Writing activities that deepen the students' understanding of biblical themes and require them to synthesize the materials include the following:

• questions for an interview with a person involved in the exile or someone who witnessed the raising of the son of the widow of Naim, or someone who was shipwrecked with Paul

• a homily focusing on a biblical theme for a Sunday Mass. (One student of mine actually had her parish priest deliver the homily she wrote on the Good Shepherd—to the delight of the parishioners.)

• a sixty-second reflection that could be given in a dial-a-message program

• all forms of poems on biblical subjects (See samples in Illustration M in Appendix.)

• an edition of a newspaper *(The Israeli Daily, The Jerusalem Journal)* centered on a major event in salvation history like the flood, the Exodus, the exile, the return to Jerusalem, the raising of Lazarus, the crucifixion, or the Resurrection. One of my students composed an edition of the *Desert Herald*. The front page article described Moses striking the rock twice. Articles included a weather report (a sandstorm), a traffic death (a pedestrian mysteriously struck down by a hit and run camel), obituaries (the pedestrian left behind seven wives, 20 children, six sheep and two tents), and an advertisement (this page brought to you by Berstein and Berstein, best used camels in the desert). The editorial chided the Israelites for complaining to God. A unique feature was this lament in the recipe page:

"Mom, we are sick and tired of having quail and manna for breakfast, lunch and dinner! When are we going to eat regular food again?"

It was followed by creative ways to serve manna and quail for each of the three meals. After reading that, few people would forget what the Israelites ate in the desert!

17: Pray
Using the Scriptures

Archbishop John F. Whealon of Hartford, Connecticut, in an article in the September 27, 1986, issue of *America* challenged us to be "a Bible-reading, Bible-loving, Bible-quoting, Bible-living Catholic people" in order to confront the threat of fundamentalism. We can be this if we are a Bible-praying people. The Bible, the meeting-place of God and his people, not only prompts us to pray, but is replete with ready-made prayers. *The Bible Prayer Book* by Eugene S. Geissler (Ave Maria Press), which is a collection of all the prayers, songs, hymns and blessings in the Bible, is 528 pages long!

Teach your students to pray Scripture. Encourage them to adopt some of the gems in the Bible as their own, such as Psalms 23, 51, and 139 or Habakkuk's brilliant act of faith:

> *For though the fig tree blossom not*
> *nor fruit be on the vines.*
> *Though the yield of the olive fail*
> *and the terraces produce no nourishment,*
> *Though the flocks disappear from the fold*
> *and there be no herd in the stalls,*
> *Yet will I rejoice in the LORD*
> *and exult in my saving God.*
> *(Habakkuk 3:17-18)*

Write short prayers on the board taken from different books of the Bible and use them before, during, or after class. Point out how one-liners like these in the Bible often make good prayers:

"Lord, I believe. Help my unbelief" (the possessed boy's father).

"Speak, Lord. Your servant is listening" (Samuel).

"Lord, to whom shall we go? You have the words of eternal life" (Peter).

"My Lord and my God!" (Thomas).

Play songs that are musical arrangements of Scripture or reflections on scriptural verses. Invite the students to turn the songs into prayers by meditating on the words.

Use sections of the Bible for prayer activities in a lesson. Ask students to formulate petitions based on the Beatitudes, the Commandments, or the Works of Mercy. Intersperse short readings from John's account of

Jesus' last discourse with time for reflection. Substitute names in Ephesians 1:3-14 with names of students in your class. It will read like this: "Blessed be God the Father of our Lord Jesus Christ, who has blessed *Margaret* with all the spiritual blessings of heaven in Christ. Before the world was made, God chose *Michael* in Christ, to be holy and spotless, and to live through love in his presence,..."(JB)

For a deeper appreciation of God's personal love for them, have the students substitute their names for "you" in Isaiah 43:1-5. Pray parts of Psalm 136 and then invite the students to add lines that merit the response "his love is everlasting." It should end up something like this:

> Give thanks to Yahweh, for he is good,
> >   his love is everlasting!
> He alone performs great marvels,
> >   his love is everlasting.
> His wisdom made the heavens,
> >   his love is everlasting.
> He led his people through the wilderness,
> >   his love is everlasting.
> He remembered us when we were down,
> >   his love is everlasting.
> He brought my lost puppy back,
> >   his love is everlasting.
> He gave us beautiful weather today,
> >   his love is everlasting.
> He helped me pass a math test,
> >   his love is everlasting.
> >   (Adapted from Psalm 136 JB)

Have the students sit quietly and page through a gospel from beginning to end, letting the headings bring to mind the events in Christ's life. Encourage them to reflect quietly on this overview in the presence of Jesus.

Introduce the scriptural rosary. Before each Hail Mary, read a line from Scripture about the decade's mystery:

For the **Joyful Mysteries,** these would be appropriate:
>   Annunciation: Luke 1:26-38
>   Visitation: Luke 1:39-56
>   Birth of Jesus: Luke 2:1-20; Philippians 2:6,7
>   Presentation: Luke 2:22-32
>   Finding of Jesus in the Temple: Luke 2:41-50

For the **Sorrowful Mysteries,** use these verses:
>   Agony in the Garden: Matthew 26:36-46
>   Scourging: Matthew 26-67; 27:20-26
>   Crowning with Thorns: Matthew 27:27-30; Philippians 2:8-11
>   Carrying of the Cross: John 19:12-17
>   Crucifixion: Matthew 27:45-54

For the **Glorious Mysteries,** use the following:
    Resurrection: Matthew 28:1-10; Mark 16:2-7
    Ascension: Matthew 28:16-20; Acts 1:10,11
    Descent of the Holy Spirit: Acts 2:1-11; 41, 42
    Assumption: Luke 1:41-50
    Crowning of Mary as Queen of Heaven: Revelation 12:1-2

As a variation, substitute other events drawn from Christ's life for the traditional fifteen mysteries.

Teach students to meditate using the following method:

Still the body: Have them still their mouths, hands, and feet. Ask older students to refrain from jiggling their feet nervously. Tell younger ones to have listening hands and feet. Have them close their eyes. Adolescents will feel freer if you stand in the back of the room. Enter into the meditation with the class, but don't close *your* eyes.

Quiet the mind: Tell them to focus on God, present here, loving them, waiting to speak to them.

Read the scriptural passage.

Recreate the story in the imagination: Guide them through it again, suggesting insights, offering descriptions.

Reflect on the story: Make it personal. Be a facilitator. Ask questions.

Respond to the Scripture: Let this take the form of a resolution or prayer. Lead the students into this by questions. Suggest topics of conversation. (See the sample meditation based on the story of Zacchaeus in Illustration N in Appendix.)

"Zacchaeus Climbs a Tree" from *Reconciliation and Penance*

18: Simulate Biblical Events

To give the students a feeling for how some of the books of the Bible were written, let them pretend to be inspired writers today. Have them select an audience and a message it needs to hear. Help them decide on a form, then let them write the message and deliver it.

Maybe you've seen the Holy Land mapped out in Chautauqua, New York, on the shore of Lake Chautauqua. In a similar manner, you can have your class create Palestine on the playground with chalk and then play out events like the Exodus and the Exile.

With preparation and planning, your students could hold a Seder meal. The meaning of Passover will be more firmly entrenched in their minds, and they will have a better understanding of the Jewish people. Perhaps you can invite a Jewish person or a Rabbi to assist with your Seder meal. (The complete English service with directions is in the booklet *Haggadah for the American Family*, published by Haggadah Institute, Merion Station, PA 19066.)

Secure volunteers to provide matzos, salt, parsley or lettuce, horseradish, charoses (a mixture of chopped apple, nuts, and cinnamon moistened with wine), grape juice, plates, and dishes. Candles and flowers will make the table more festive.

You might wish to prepare the special Seder plate of symbolic foods: bitter herbs (horseradish), a vegetable (parsley or lettuce), a more bitter vegetable (radish), charoses, a bone, and a hard-boiled egg. Inform the students that the egg is a symbol of the sacrifices offered at the Temple. The other foods are explained during the service itself.

Before the Passover meal, tell the students that they will drink from the cup four times because of the fourfold promise the Lord made to the Israelites: "I will bring you forth," "I will deliver you," "I will redeem you," and "I will take you." Also explain that the extra cup of wine on the table is for Elijah, the prophet who is to announce the day of universal peace and love on his return. (See Illustration O in Appendix for an adapted version of the Seder meal ritual.)

19: Collect Bible-Related Materials

If you have avid collectors of baseball cards, stickers, and record albums, transform them into collectors of biblical items. Throughout your scriptural studies, encourage your students to watch for newspaper and magazine articles on the Bible. These can be shared with the class and then posted. Have the students be on the lookout for references to the Bible on TV, over the radio, on billboards, or in books. They can record these references in their notebooks and then report them to the class.

Have the students make scrapbooks: a scrapbook about Israel complete with illustrations, or a scrapbook on a particular book of the Bible. As an alternative, let students collect objects in a shoebox. A Genesis shoebox might contain such things as an article on how the universe began, a plastic apple, a button that says, "I belong to God," a rainbow magnet, a poem about Abraham, an English-French pocket dictionary, and a picture of a pyramid.

As a culminating project, students could assemble a booklet of their favorite passages in the Bible interspersed with pictures and/or drawings. Another possibility is to have them make a prayerbook of biblical prayers.

As an ongoing activity, students could collect biblical terms and produce a dictionary. They can illustrate the entries to make a picture dictionary. This last can be a class project with each student volunteering to do one or more of the pages.

20: Use Programmed Learning for Efficient Learning

Granted the goal of biblical study is not so much information as transformation, yet there is a definite body of knowledge we want students to master. The best way I know to teach many facts and concepts fast and well is programmed learning, a form of independent study. There are arguments against it, but the strongest argument for it is that it works.

In programmed learning, concepts are presented in frames which the students read by themselves, using a cover sheet and revealing one frame at a time. As they progress through the lessson acquiring new bits of knowledge, they meet questions about information from previous frames. The answer to each question appears in the next frame for immediate feedback. The frames can be set in two columns so that the students fold the sheet in half and go down one column at a time.

Background information on the Bible is one area that can be taught by programmed learning. Here is an example that illustrates what kind of material goes in each frame:

"Bible " comes from a Greek word for book.

The Bible is a collection of books written between 1400 B.C. and 100 A.D. The primary author of the Bible is God, so the Bible is sacred.

There are two main divisions in the Bible. The Hebrew Scriptures are written mostly in Hebrew and contain 46 books.
   —What does "bible" mean?

The New Testament was written mainly in Greek and contains 27 books.
   —Who is the primary author of the Bible?
                        BOOK

The church determined which books belong to the Bible. Catholics accept more books in Hebrew Scripture than the Jewish people and Protestants.
   —How many books are in the Hebrew Scriptures?
                        GOD

The Hebrew Scriptures tell the history of Israel, God's chosen people.
—Who determined what books belong to the Bible?

46

The New Testament tells the story of Christ and his church.
—How many books are in the New Testament?

THE CHURCH

We say that God inspired the Bible. This means that God directed the minds and wills of the human authors to write what God wished to reveal.
—Which part of the Bible tells the history of Israel?

27

The Bible is also called Sacred Scripture. "Scripture" means writings. The Bible contains many forms of writing such as letters, poetry, short stories, and prayers.
—Why is God the primary author of the Bible?

HEBREW SCRIPTURES

In order to understand a book of the Bible, it helps to know its form. Davy Crockett, the frontiersman, really existed, but his killing a bear when he was three-years-old is part of a legend about him. Similarly, some biblical stories are not meant to be taken literally.
—What does the New Testament tell about?

GOD INSPIRED IT

The Bible is not meant to teach historical or scientific truth. Its truth lies in what it reveals about God and our relationship with God
—What does it mean to say that God inspired the Bible?

CHRIST AND THE CHURCH

The church, the believing community, has the power to interpret the Bible correctly.
—Must everything in the Bible be accepted as fact?

GOD DIRECTED THE MINDS AND WILLS OF THE HUMAN AUTHORS TO WRITE WHAT GOD WISHED TO REVEAL

NO

This method is good for variety, and the students like it, especially if it is introduced as a chance for them to teach themselves. Tests given shortly afterwards usually yield high scores and give the students much personal satisfaction.

David S. Strickler

21: Play
Bible Games

Lead children into Scripture through play. Be alert for biblical crossword puzzles and word searches. (See Illustrations A and P in Appendix.) Invent your own puzzles and games. Invest in books or publications for religious educators that contain ideas for making scriptural study fun.

To lighten review lessons, cut up pictures of biblical stories and have the children piece the puzzle together and identify the story. With older students pin names of biblical persons on the backs of individuals and have them ask their classmates yes and no questions until they figure out who they are. Challenge the class with riddles, maybe even in the form of poems.

To review biblical terms, play "Vocab." Have the students set up their papers like Bingo cards with V-O-C-A-B across the top and a free space in the middle. Instruct them to write a term or name from the unit to be reviewed in each block. Prepare a set of cards with the same terms. Distribute markers to each student. As each term is drawn from the cards, a student must identify it. Students who have that term on their cards cover it with a marker. The game proceeds until someone has "Vocab."

Here are some possible terms for a unit on Israel's kings:

Samuel	Goliath	Absalom	Abner
Saul	temple	Nathan	Jesse
David	psalms	Bathsheba	Jerusalem
Solomon	proverbs	wisdom	Bethlehem
monarchy	Jonathan	Ark of the Covenant	shepherd
anoint	Philistine	Israel	obedience

To provide practice in looking up scriptural references, hold a contest. Distribute a sheet of ten questions with the scriptural references that contain the answer to each. Make the questions interesting, for example:

1. Who made clothes for Adam and Eve?—(*Genesis 3:21*)
2. How old was Moses when he asked Pharoah to let the Israelites go?
   —(*Exodus 7:7*)
3. What kind of person says there is no God?—(*Psalms 53:1*)
4. A lovely woman who is rebellious is like what?—(*Proverbs 11:22*)
5. What animals did David kill singlehandedly?—(*1 Samuel 17:36*)
6. What did Amos call the wealthy ladies of Israel?—(*Amos 4:1*)
7. What did Jesus say we must make our home?—(*John 8:31*)
8. Who let Peter out of prison?—(*Acts 12:7*)

9. How many times was Paul whipped for being a Christian?—(2 Corinthians 11:24)
10. What does the Bible ask Jesus to do at its close?— (Revelation 22:20)

The first one to find the answers to all ten questions wins. In case you're wondering, here are the answers:

1)	Yahweh	6)	cows
2)	eighty	7)	his Word
3)	a fool	8)	an angel
4)	a golden ring in the snout of a pig	9)	195 (5 times 39)
5)	a lion and a bear	10)	come

To involve your whole school or religious education program in biblical games, plan a *Bible Bazaar* with your students. Let them brainstorm to organize booths and activities related to the Bible. Money collected can be donated to an organization that works for social justice to fulfill the injunctions of biblical prophets like Amos. Prizes for any of the games could be biblical, e.g., a Bible, a cake decorated like a Bible, an album of biblical songs. You might use some of these starter ideas for your Bible Bazaar activities:

• A word search for the participants as they enter (See Illustration A in Appendix.)

• A booth where stones, buttons, and plaques with scriptural quotations lettered on them are sold

• the presentation of a short play about a biblical story

• A Jacob's Well fishpond where Jonah's whales are caught

• Instant Bingo in which players draw folded papers containing scriptural references and then look them up to see if they match any of the winning verses that are posted

• A Wise Man's booth where a correct answer to a question on the Bible entitles the player to a chance on a large prize

• A penny pitch game in which players toss pennies, trying to land on the "promised land"

• A Spread-the-Word booth for attaching scriptural messages to helium balloons and releasing them into the sky

22: Set Up Learning Stations with Scripture Activities

A teaching technique that students find exciting is learning stations. For a topic to be studied, think of five or six short and varied activities. Set up a station in the room for each activity. Mark it with a large number and supply it with directions and materials needed to carry out the activity. Explain to the students the general idea of each activity and give them each a card indicating the order in which they are to move from station to station. At definite time intervals, give a signal for the students to move to their next station.

Here is a set of activities for learning stations on the Book of Psalms:

STATION 1:—The students study information on the psalms from a sheet of paper. When they are ready, one of them dictates an oral quiz from a card in an envelope.

Sheet: The psalms are the song-prayers of Israel collected over a period of 700 years. Some of the 150 psalms are believed to have been written by King David who was skilled at playing the harp. The psalms are a book of the Bible situated approximately in the middle of the Hebrew Scriptures. As God's inspired Word, they are a living source of power.

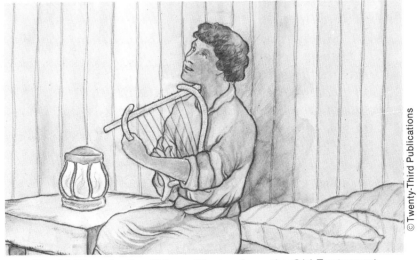

"David Plays for Saul" from *Stories from the Old Testament*

The psalms have many purposes. They praise and thank God, ask for God's help or forgiveness, and ask for blessings on the leaders of the land.

Some psalms remind people of how God acted to save them, and some encourage them to follow God's law. Certain verses of the "messianic psalms" can be interpreted to apply to Jesus.

The psalms were the official prayer of Israel used in the Temple service. They were the prayers of Jesus and Mary. Today, the psalms are still popular prayers. Psalm 8 is the "moon psalm" quoted in connection with the Apollo 8 flight. We pray and sing the psalms at Mass. Every day priests, religious, and other Christians pray the Liturgy of the Hours, which is composed mainly of psalms. Many people like to pray the psalms as personal prayer. Perhaps you, too, will learn to love and pray the psalms.

Quiz: 1. *What are psalms?*
       2. *How many are there?*
       3. *Who wrote some of them?*
       4. *What are the purposes of the psalms?*

STATION 2:—The students recite psalms in three different ways:

• A leader recites Psalm 46 while the rest repeat the antiphon after each verse.

• The group divides into two and recites Psalm 98, alternating verses.

• The entire group recites Psalm 150 together.

STATION 3:—The students listen to a psalm set to music and watch accompanying slides (if possible).

STATION 4:—The students design a bookmark from a psalm verse, choosing from this list:

> *My God, my rock of refuge* (Ps. 18:3).
> *The heavens declare the glory of God* (Ps. 19:2).
> *Beside restful waters God leads me* (Ps. 23:2).
> *God guides me in right paths* (Ps. 23:3).
> *Be glad in the* Lord *and rejoice, you just* (Ps. 32:11).
> *God made firm my steps* (Ps. 40:3).
> *My joy lies in being close to God* (Ps. 73:28 JB).
> *You are the God who works wonders* (Ps. 77:15).
> *Your love for me has been so great* (Ps. 86:13 JB).
> *I mean to sing to Yahweh all my life* (Ps. 104:33 JB).
> *God's love is everlasting* (Ps. 107:1 JB).

STATION 5:—The students write their own psalms using as a model Psalm 5, 8, 23, 136, or another short psalm. (See Chapter 8, *Rewrite*.)

STATION 6:—The students match psalm verses with human feelings.

—When I am frightened because people are attacking me...

—When I am worried...

—When I am at peace...

—When I am in awe at God's power...

—When I feel guilty...

—When I am grateful to God...

—When I am happy because of God's love for me...

> A. Ps. 23; B. Ps. 69:14-17; C. Ps. 138; D. Ps.47:1-7;
> E. Ps.131; F. Ps. 51:1-11; G. Ps. 145

> *Answers may vary: B, A, E, G, F, C, D*

Other topics that can be taught by means of learning stations are the Exodus, wisdom books, the prophets, Jesus' miracles, Jesus' teachings, and the New Testament letters.

23: Use Audiovisuals to Spark Bible Studies

Today there are many fine audiovisuals with biblical themes on the market. Students will enjoy *Stories from the Old Testament*, filmstrips published by Twenty-Third Publications. Part I An Awakening People (creation, Adam and Eve, Cain and Abel, Noah); Part II A Faithful People (Abraham, Joseph); Part III A Covenant People (Moses, the Exodus); Part IV A Kingdom People (Saul, David, Solomon); Part V A Prophetic People (Overview of prophets, Jeremiah, Ezekiel).

There are also movies such as *The Bible, Jacob and Joseph, Jesus of Nazareth, Jesus Christ Superstar,* and *Godspell.* Most of these are available as videocassettes. Tabor Publishing (P.O. Box 7000, Allen, TX 75002) is currently offering videocassettes of biblical stories from Hanna-Barbera's animated film *The Greatest Adventure.* Some of the popular Arch Books also have been transformed into videocassettes by The Liturgical Press (Collegeville, MN 56321).

Perhaps you're one of those people who hesitate to use projectors of any kind. If this is the case, find someone else to operate the equipment for you, but don't deprive your students of audiovisuals. With a preview and a follow-up discussion or activity, an AV program can be a memorable learning experience. Films, videos, filmstrips, and other commercially produced programs are most worthwhile when they are chosen with care to fit the lesson. Don't just use them as a last resort because your lesson isn't planned!

Take advantage of biblical movies and programs on television by calling the students' attention to them. To motivate the students to watch these, offer extra credit for a brief report.

Also involve your students by having them make audiovisual aids like the following:

• Figures for the flannel board made out of flannel or from paper with a piece of flannel glued to the back

• A scroll of pictures for the opaque projector using student drawings, magazine pictures, or both

• A recording of a biblical passage with background music and an introduction

• Slides of clay or paper representations of scenes from a biblical story

- Slides made with supplies like "Write-On" from Kodak. Special projection pens allow the slides to be erased and reused

- Do-it-yourself filmstrips. Kits for this can be purchased from Rorer Group, Inc.; 1450 East Brooks Rd; Memphis, TN 38116. (See Illustration Q in Appendix for filmstrip frames on Jonah.)

- A homemade movie, if the necessary video equipment is available

- Transparencies or cutout figures for an overhead presentation

"Jeremiah Confronts Hananiah" from *Stories from the Old Testament*

Students can present a unique demonstration of creation on the overhead in this manner:

1. The program opens with a pyrex dish filled with water on the overhead and a cutout dove (the Spirit) above it.

2. The water is blown from the side to represent the mighty wind that swept over the water.

3. An Alka-Seltzer is dropped into the water to give the impression of creative action.

4. A sheet of paper masks one half of the screen on a diagonal to show the division of light and darkness.

5. Drops of blue food coloring in the bottom of the dish represent the division of water.

6. Transparencies show the rest of the days of creation. These are made by cutting away forms from paper and then backing the figures that remain

in the sheet with pieces of colored cellophane. (See Illustration R in Appendix.)

As a background to this, one of my classes used a recording of Charlton Heston reading the creation account from Genesis. At the times when the reading was broken by a song, a cut-glass bowl was rotated above the overhead, casting lovely designs of light on the screen.

Any concrete object related to a topic can reinforce a lesson. For example, a sand dollar can be a lead into a lesson on the crucifixion. For a dramatic introduction to Jeremiah who prophesied through symbolic actions, shatter an inexpensive earthenware jar in front of the class—far enough away so that no one is hurt. Bring a packet of seeds to class when teaching about the sower or the mustard seed.

Challenge the students to assemble a multimedia presentation as a culminating activity. They can combine live or recorded music, slides (perhaps from their own homes), filmstrips, and transparencies in any number of ways to create a powerful lesson.

David Strickler

24: Computerize Bible Lessons

To put some wine into new wineskins, so to speak, make use of the computer to teach biblical concepts. More and more programs are being produced commercially. Some recent ones are the following:

• *Bible Learning 1-2-3*, Baker Book House, P.O. Box 6287, Grand Rapids, MI 49506, Apple. Commodore. (Biblical stories are acted out by the Baker Street kids. Questions for recall, understanding and discovery follow.)

• *Bible Stories* Friar Tech Software. Available from Silver Burdett Co., 250 James St., Morristown, NJ 07960, Apple. Commodore. Atari. (Primary and intermediate children are taught the stories of Noah's Ark, the Ten Commandments, and the Beatitudes.)

• *BIK*, Bible Instruction Komputer, As Jesus Taught, Inc., 320 East Ripa Ave, St. Louis, MO 63125, Grades 1-3: Commodore 64 - 128. Grades 4-8: Commodore 64 - 128. Apple II. (This computer-managed instructional system when completed will be comprised of eight sets of five units (five-to-ten lessons each) in the following sequence: grade 1 — Creation and the coming of Jesus; grade 2 — The last days of Jesus; grade 3 — The parables; grade 4 — The miracles; grade 5 — The living, ethical messages of Jesus; grade 6 — The Eucharist; grade 7 — The Holy Spirit; grade 8 — The Church in Acts and in the Vatican documents.)

• *Right Again*, Ascension Designs. Distributed by Rainfall, Inc., 1534 College, S.E., Grand Rapids, MI 49508. Apple II. Commodore 64. (Children eight years and older identify persons, places, and things from the Old Testament.)

• *Test Creator*, Friar Tech Software. Available from Silver Burdett Co., 250 James St., Morristown, NJ 07960, Apple. Commodore. (This program produces multiple choice, true-or-false, and fill-in tests.)

T.E.S.S. The Educational Software Selector lists under "religious education" other software that teach biblical stories and that drill biblical facts, the order of the books, and the location of biblical places. One program containing the complete text of the King James Bible bears the clever title "The Word Processor."

You might try creating your own computer programs to teach, review, and test material on the Bible. A word of caution: Avoid programs that spend much more time on games than on actual tasks.

25: Celebrate Sacred Scripture

This past year I met a convert of a year and a half. She was an attractive women with three teenaged children. She had shopped around for a religion and had decided on Catholicism. She explained, "I chose to be a Catholic because of the way they celebrate the Word."

The rituals, the gestures, songs, and prayers of a celebration sink deep down into the heart of a child. Celebrations make us realize profound realities. They form convictions and shape attitudes. It is important to celebrate the Word with our students. One ideal time for a celebration of the Bible is National Bible week, which is observed annually from the Sunday before Thanksgiving to the Sunday after Thanksgiving.

Catechists concerned about covering content might feel guilty taking time for such a celebration. They should think of it, however, as a lesson on liturgy. For, as Romano Guardini said, "The liturgy does not wish to achieve anything, but merely wants to dwell in the presence of God, to breathe and unfold, to love and praise him." The *Constitution on the Sacred Liturgy* encourages celebrations that help the children to understand some of the elements of the liturgy. It states: "Such celebrations can do much to enhance their appreciation of the Word of God" (14).

If students receive personal copies of the Bible for use during the year, why not present them in a special ceremony? Possibly a priest or other guest could give a talk on Scripture, bless the Bibles, and then distribute them. The distribution makes more of an impact if each student is called by name, presented with the Bible, and exhorted to hear God's Word and keep it. Appropriate prayers, readings, and songs can be chosen to enrich the celebration.

In other celebrations, honor the Bible by carrying it in procession, holding it high, and enthroning it. The sacredness of the Bible is conveyed to the children when we handle it with reverence. The classroom Bible can be kept open on a stand throughout the year. Flowers and candles can be placed near it as symbols of the life and light the Word of God is for us.

A good culminating activity for a unit is a prayer service that incorporates scriptural readings and time for reflection on the Word. The students can help plan it. (See Illustration S in Appendix for a prayer service on the Word of God itself. Its simple format can be followed for other topics.)

26: Apply God's Word to Life

We can't give students what we don't have. We must encounter God's Word working in our hearts if we wish to touch the lives of our children. The best way to lead students to a love and knowledge of Scripture is to assign it an important role in our own lives. Reading the Bible, praying it, and reflecting over it, we come to value it. Only then are we able to communicate that sense of value to those we teach.

If we believe that God speaks to us today through Scripture, we will read it from the perspective of our own situations. We will draw parallels with our own lives and be nourished by the Word. The following is a reflection on the Book of Jonah as seen through the eyes of a catechist. It is an attempt to relate Scripture to our very real and present situations.

Jonah, Patron of Catechists

For too long the prophet Jonah has been overshadowed (or swallowed up?) by the great fish that swam into his life. Granted, this fish with the cast-iron stomach is an important supporting character in the tale. But when measured by instruments other than yardsticks, a person is bigger than a fish.

Anyone not distracted by the whale will realize that Jonah is a prime candidate for the role of patron of catechists. He is no super-hero like Abraham, Moses, or David. He does not stride across the pages of the Bible in sandals too large for the average Christian to wear. He does not possess a secret weapon (like Samson's hair). Nor does he have to withstand a hundred and one forms of persecution as Jeremiah did. All in all, Jonah is an ordinary man living an ordinary prophet's life.

Jonah, utterly and pitifully human in his faults and foibles, goes about his noble task of prophesying, showing fear, anger, obstinacy, and unpredictability. And yet, God uses him to accomplish the impossible. Because of Jonah's flawed but successful service, he offers hope to every aspiring catechist who is less than perfect.

The story of Jonah opens with God's command to him to march into Nineveh, the capital of Israel's dreaded enemy Assyria. His mission: to preach against Nineveh and to predict that in forty days it would be wiped off the face of the earth—a job comparable to condemning communism in the streets of Moscow. Any catechist assigned to spread the Good News to a class that has the reputation of being bad news should have no trouble identifying with Jonah.

Jonah does not take the time to go through a process of discernment or to consult his spiritual director. He does the natural, cowardly thing. He runs away. Jonah is so terrified that simply refusing to cooperate is not enough. He boards a ship bound for the faraway city of Tarshish.

Jonah's goodness, however, redeems him. First of all, as the Bible points out, he pays the fare on the escape ship. He is not a stowaway. Further, he honestly and humbly, if not prudently, admits to the crew that he is fleeing from his God.

All goes well for the runaway prophet until a raging storm attacks the ship. So violent is this storm that the sailors toss the cargo overboard to lighten the ship. Somehow, in the midst of keeping the ship afloat, the crew finds time to cast lots to see who is to blame for the weather. Of course, the lots accuse Jonah. Unaware that the Lord is closing in on him, our hero lies fast asleep in the hold. Quite a feat considering the thunder, the waves, and his conscience, but it is characteristically human.

Once prodded awake and apprised of the situation, Jonah proves himself a really good Joe. He suggests that the sailors dump him overboard to save themselves and the ship. They take his advice and what follows is a conversion worthy of the *Guiness Book of Records*. When the storm clears, all the sailors worship Jonah's God, the God who made the sea and the land.

Leaving Jonah in the sea for awhile, let us consider the manner of his shipboard witness. He does not preach a word to the sailors, but surrenders his life for their sakes. Through his self-sacrifice, the tough pagan sailors come to a knowledge of God. Ironically, when Jonah—a coward, a jinx, and an outcast—most looks and feels like a total failure, he succeeds.

Now for the only "fishy" part of the Jonah tale. While Jonah flounders in the swirling waters, seaweed clinging about his head, the Lord sends a large fish to catch him. Notice that the whale's obedience to the Lord in the face of an unpleasant task exceeds that of Jonah. But who can surpass Jonah's trust in the Lord when he prays a prayer of thanksgiving—not an act of contrition—from the belly of this fish. Again, Jonah shows himself the perfect model for catechists.

Although in dire straits, half-drowned, and eaten by a sea monster (and what catechist has never been in a similar position?), Jonah is still full of living faith and praise for God. Living up to Jonah's confidence in him, the Lord delivers Jonah, via whale express, from ship to shore. There Jonah is spewed out safe and sound, though probably a bit shaken and seasick.

After his little game of hide-and-seek, Jonah is ready for Nineveh. His drenching has called him to his senses, and he realizes that the Lord's will for him might well be the least of many possible evils.

Once in Nineveh, after only a single day of prophesying doom, Jonah surely merits the prophet-of-the-year award. For everyone in the city, including the king, fasts and sits in sackcloth and ashes. Even the sheep and cattle fast and wear sackcloth in sympathy with their masters, making the fields of Nineveh a sight to behold.

What was Jonah's secret? He was not a prophet of many words or the book named for him would be longer than four chapters. According to the Bible, his words were not accompanied by spine-tingling miracles. And he certainly did not bombard the Ninevites through the media. Except in a passive way, the mass conversion of Nineveh was not Jonah's doing at all. It was God's. When Jonah finally let God use him, great things happened. Literally, he was an overnight success. God was able to work through Jonah to save an entire city. Jonah learns that being a witness is being a tool in the hands of God. God speaks and acts through people who turn over their lives to him.

The proper place for the story to end would be right here with God so moved by the people's repentance that he decides to cancel their punishment. God's prophet, Jonah, is covered in glory. But the foolish, unpredictable side of Jonah's human nature crops up and prolongs the tale.

Instead of being thrilled at Nineveh's overwhelmingly positive response to his message, Jonah is angry that God changed his mind about destroying the city. He had been rather looking forward to seeing a spectacular fire and brimstone demolition of his enemy. Therefore, Jonah breaks into a complaining speech in which he pretends that he fled before only because he knew that God was going to forgive the Ninevites.

Strangely, in the course of his tantrum, Jonah pays God a memorable compliment when he says, "I knew that you are a gracious and merciful God, slow to anger, rich in clemency, loathe to punish." Jonah concludes by declaring that he is so angry, he wants to die. After his outburst, the disgruntled man parks himself on the outskirts of the town to see if God will comply with his wishes and consume Nineveh.

What happens next is a lesson for catechists as well as for Jonah. The divine teacher prepares a concrete learning experience for his thickheaded and hardhearted prophet. In one day a shady gourd plant springs up to protect Jonah from the hot sun. The following day a hungry worm chomps on the plant and kills it. Jonah gets just as angry about the plant as he did about Nineveh. With that, God draws the moral from the withered plant. Jonah is concerned about one gourd plant. Softening the lesson with gentle humor, God asks, "And should I not be concerned over Nineveh, the great city, in which there are more than a hundred and twenty thousand persons who cannot distinguish their right hand from their left, not to mention the many cattle?"

Jonah apparently is speechless, for the story abruptly ends with that question. No doubt, knowing the value of personal life stories in his work, Jonah repeated the story of Nineveh over and over during the remaining years of his ministry. Now almost three thousand years later, Jonah's tale, as a book of the Bible, is still influencing people's lives.

Although he is sometimes called the comic relief of the Bible, Jonah is undeniably a man of no small stature. Later another prophet (who could also sleep through storms at sea), compared Jonah's three-day imprisonment in the whale to his own confinement in a tomb. Ever since then Jonah has been a sign and witness of the Resurrection.

What more could we ask of the patron of catechists?

Joanne Meldrum

APPENDIX OF ILLUSTRATIONS

Bible Book Search

NAME:_____ Total found: _____

The names of all the books in the Bible are hidden in the square below. They are horizontal, vertical, or diagonal. When you find one, circle it and cross it off the list. Books with the same name appear only once.

```
L O X B E L T U J P H I L E M O N M R C O I V
G A L A T I A N S E S T R P X I L E T O B I T
N U M B E R S O C M R I D H S O T V X L N O C
B A J E E K N Q L U K E S E R E D S I O B I F
O C H H N V I A X N O E M S P A L O T S H T S
P T T U A T S E C C L E S I A S T E S S Y E G
L S V T M P A O G C I H K A A Z H Q T I M S E
E O J X I Y P T I E J O B N M H E Z R A X I R
V F U L R M R N I Y N S V S I O S X J N E N O
I T D S U J O E L O G E C D P G S W I S D O M
T H I F T R V T B Z N A S L N R A N V L M X A
I E T T H N E C H O C S I I X D L J E K M B N
C A H C U O R H E Y I A K P S T O I M X A T S
U P R A L S B I X O G Z E P H A N I A H T L D
S O N G O F S O N G S B U I K A I H S C T Q I
N S I R E V E L A T I O N O D J A R A X H I Z
E T I S Q X A H Z D E U T E R O N O M Y E P E
H L P M A R K Y A S T H F L A H S N U F W Y C
E E C O R I N T H I A N S M Z N S T E N I X H
M S B V O A A P H I L I P P I A N S L H J C A
I K X R U I Y H D O X Q U R A C X J C I U T R
A C U H E T M A S I R A C H O W A A U R D N I
H E S I F W B R Y P E Z E K I E L H A D G U A
J O N A H O S H A B A K K U K A L B I T E P H
J A D M A C C A B E E S G X M O Q A K E S O L
```

Genesis
Exodus
Leviticus
Numbers
Deuteronomy
Joshua
Judges
Ruth

Samuel 1, 2
Kings 1, 2
Chronicles 1, 2
Ezra
Nehemiah
Tobit
Judith
Esther
Maccabees 1, 2

Job
Psalms
Proverbs
Ecclesiastes
Song of Songs
Wisdom
Sirach

Isaiah
Jeremiah
Lamentations
Baruch
Ezekiel
Daniel
Hosea
Joel
Amos
Obadiah
Jonah
Micah
Nahum
Habakkuk

Matthew
Mark
Luke
John & epistles 1, 2, 3
Acts of the Apostles
Romans
Corinthians 1, 2

Galatians
Ephesians
Philippians
Colossians
Thessalonians 1, 2
Timothy 1, 2
Titus

Philemon
Hebrews
James
Peter 1, 2
Jude
Revelation

Zephaniah
Haggai
Zechariah
Malachi

(Answers are on following page.)

Answers to Bible Book Search

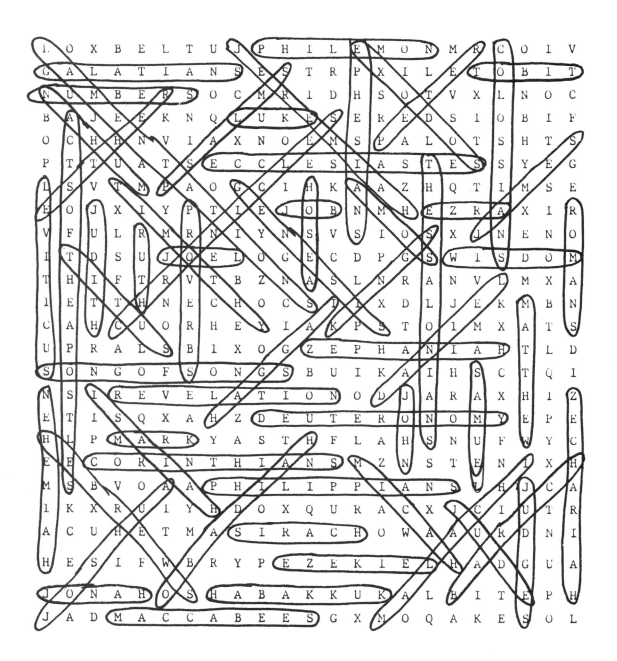

Israel's Greatest King
(I Samuel 16-18:16,26)

Not living up to his God-given call
Was the Israelites' first king, a man named _____.   *(Saul)*
So Samuel looked for a new king for them
Among Jesse's eight sons, town of _____.   *(Bethlehem)*
Who to anoint? Little thought Samuel gave it.
He chose the youngest, none other than _____.   *(David)*

He was handsome and strong; the Lord's law he did keep.
The boy was called in from tending the _____.   *(sheep)*
When King Saul grew moody and sorely depressed,
His friends told him David could cure him the best.
He could sing and compose; his mind was quite sharp.
So David soothed Saul with his songs on the _____.   *(harp)*

"Let just one man fight me and if he should dieth,
You all lose," daily cried the giant _____.   *(Goliath)*
For God's army, David accepted the dare.
Guarding sheep he had killed both a lion and a _____.   *(bear)*

No other armor than God's help he got.
His weapon: five stones and his trusty _____.   *(slingshot)*
In seconds the boy had Goliath quite dead:
Slung a stone to his forehead, then cut off his _____.   *(head)*

David, a hero because of that deed,
Next was appointed Saul's army to _____.   *(lead)*
His victories soon outdid Saul's former feats,
And people began to cheer him in the _____.   *(streets)*
On hearing the shouts Saul with jealousy was filled,
Tried twice with his spear to have David _____.   *(killed)*
David wandered the land with the king close behind
Until something one night changed angry Saul's _____.   *(mind)*

As Saul lay asleep with his spear at his head,
David could easily have killed *him* instead.
But he warned his men not to attack,
Just stole the spear, and then quietly moved _____.   *(back)*
The next morning Saul said, "You're more upright than I."
And decided to let all the hard feelings die.
Because toward God's leader David did the right thing.
He himself lived to become Israel's greatest _____.   *(king)*

Illustration C

Chalk Talk for the Prodigal Son

A Play About Queen Esther

Cast
Narrator
King Ahasuerus
Queen Vashti
Esther

Mordecai
Haman
Town Crier
Servant 1

Servant 2
Advisor
Maid

SCENE ONE

(The palace. Ahasuerus, Haman, and the advisor are dining. Servant 1 stands nearby. Vashti is apart from them in her room.)

Narrator King Ahasuerus held a great feast in Persia to show the wealth of his kingdom to his officials. All went well until the seventh day.

King *(to Servant 1)* Go tell Queen Vashti to come here so everyone can see her beauty. *(Servant bows and leaves.)*

Servant 1 *(to Vashti)* Your royal highness, his majesty commands you to appear before his guests.

Vashti I don't feel like going. Tell the king I will not come.

Servant 1 *(bowing to king)* My Lord, the Queen will not come.

(Haman and advisor gasp.)

King *(angrily)* How dare she refuse? What shall be done to punish her disobedience to a royal order?

Advisor Queen Vashti has wronged you and the kingdom. When other women hear of this, they will imitate her. Issue a decree of divorce and find a more worthy queen.

King Yes, I think I must.

(All exit.)

Town Crier Hear ye. hear ye! The disobedient Vashti is no longer queen of Persia. Let all beautiful maidens be brought to the palace. The one who most pleases the king will become queen.

SCENE TWO

(Two servants and Mordecai stand on the road.)

Narrator Mordecai, a Jew, had adopted his cousin Esther, a lovely girl. Of all the women who came to the palace, Ahasuerus chose Esther to be queen. He did not know that she was Jewish. Then the king made Haman his highest official and ordered all to bow to him when he passed.

(Haman approaches.)

Servant 1 Here comes Haman. *(Servants bow.)*

Servant 2 *(to Mordecai)* Everyday when Haman comes by, you stand. Why do you disobey the king?

Mordecai I bow to God alone. *(Exits)*

Servant 1 *(to Haman)* My Lord, there is a man who refuses to bow to you.

Haman What! Who is he?

Servant 2 The Jew, Mordecai.

Haman I'll wipe those stiffnecked people off the face of the earth.

(Servants exit. Haman goes to king.)

Haman Your majesty, in your kingdom there is a people who do not obey your laws. Issue a decree to destroy them, and I'll add ten thousand silver pieces to the treasury.

King Keep your money, but here is my official seal. Do what you want.

(They exit.)

Town Crier Hear ye. Hear ye! The king decrees: Haman, second only to me and whom I look upon as a father, has warned me. In his wisdom and loyalty, he has brought to my attention a wicked people living in our kingdom. We hereby order all Jews put to death by the sword on the fourteenth day of the last month.

SCENE THREE

(Esther's room. Esther is attended by Servant 2. Mordecai is outside the palace.)

Servant 2 Your highness, Mordecai is in sackcloth and ashes and he's crying loudly.

Esther Go find out why.

Servant 2 *(to Mordecai)* The queen bids me ask why you are mourning.

Mordecai Doesn't she know that Haman had the king order all the Jewish people killed? Tell her this and instruct her to plead with the king to save us.

Servant 2 *(to Esther)* Mordecai says Haman got the king to decree that all Jews be killed. He says you must speak to the king on behalf of your people.

Esther Anyone who goes to the king without being summoned is killed on the spot unless the king extends his scepter. Tell him that.

Servant 2 *(to Mordecai)* Esther reminds you of the death penalty for those who go to the king without being sent for.

Mordecai Tell her that since she's Jewish, she will be killed with the rest of us. Maybe she became queen just to meet this crisis.

Servant 2 *(to Esther)* Mordecai says you must go or be killed, too.

Esther So be it. Tell Mordecai to have the Jews fast with me for three days. Then I will go to the king.

(Servant exits. Esther prays.)

Esther My Lord help me. Put words into my mouth to save us from the wicked. Deliver me from my fear.

SCENE FOUR

(The palace. The king is on the throne. Servant 1 is present. Esther and her maid are at the doorway.)

Narrator After three days of penance, Esther approaches the king. She was beautiful, but had to lean on a maid for support. The king looked up angrily. Esther grew faint and the king sprang from his throne.

King *(extending his scepter to Esther)* What is it, Esther? Even if you wish half my kingdom, you will have it.

Esther If it please your majesty, come tomorrow with Haman to a banquet I shall prepare.

King *(to Servant 1)* Have Haman fulfill Esther's wish.

(Servant bows and exits.)

Esther Thank you, my Lord.

SCENE FIVE

(King's inner court the next day.)

Narrator Haman's joy at the invitation was spoiled because Mordecai still refused to bow to him. His wife and friends suggested that he erect a gallows seventy-five feet high and ask the king to have

Mordecai hanged. That night the king couldn't sleep. He asked that the record of events be read to him. In the course of the reading, the king realized that once when Mordecai had saved his life, he had never been rewarded. The next morning Haman seeks to ask the king for Mordecai's death.

King   Ah, Haman. What should be done for the man the king wishes to reward?

Haman   *(aside)* He must mean me. *(to king)* He should wear the king's robe and crown and ride the king's horse. The noblest officials should clothe him and then go before him in the public square crying out, "This is what is done for the man whom the king wishes to reward."

King   Hurry. You are my noblest official. Do this for the Jew, Mordecai.

Haman   *(shocked)* As you say, O King. *(Bows and exits.)*

SCENE SIX

(Palace banquet. Ahasuerus, Esther, and Haman dine, attended by Servant 1.)

King   Whatever you ask, Queen Esther, shall be granted to you.

Esther: O King, I ask that my life and the lives of my people be spared. We have been condemned to death.

King   Who and where is this man who dared to do this?

Esther   Our enemy is this wicked Haman!

(King exits angrily to the garden. Haman goes to Esther.)

Haman   My Queen, please save me. The king is so angry he will kill me.

(King returns.)

King   Will he assault the queen in my own house?

Servant 1   Your majesty, at Haman's house is a gallows on which he planned to hang Mordecai.

King   Hang this man on it.

(Servant takes Haman away.)

King   Esther, I give you Haman's house.

Esther   I will give it to Mordecai, for he is my cousin who adopted me.

King   Then I will also give Mordecai my signet ring. You and he may write to all the provinces whatever you see fit concerning the Jews.

Narrator Thus it came to pass that the following message was proclaimed.

Town Crier Hear ye. Hear ye! Many ambitious men in high places take advantage of their position to wrong innocent people. Haman was such a man. You will do well to ignore the letter sent by him. The Jews may follow their own law. Everyone may help them defend themselves on the fourteenth day of Adar. That day must be celebrated forever.

the end

Our Father, Abraham

(A Choral Reading)

CHORUS	Yahweh spoke to Abram.
YAHWEH *(strong, deep)*	Leave your country and your father's house for the land I will show you. I will make you a great nation; I will bless you. All nations of the earth will be blessed in you.
ABRAM	I will go forth, Lord God, to a new land, to a great blessing.
CHORUS	Abram came to Canaan, the land that was promised.
YAHWEH	To your descendants I will give this land.
ABRAM *(questioning)*	But, Lord, I have no children. I am old; my wife is old.
YAHWEH	Come outside and look at the sky. Count the stars if you can. So shall your descendants be.
CHORUS	Abram put his faith in the Lord. And Yahweh made a covenant with him.
YAHWEH	Walk before me and be blameless. Your name shall be Abraham. You shall become the father of many nations.
CHORUS *(echoing)*	The father of many nations.
YAHWEH	Your descendants will be kings. I will make a covenant with them. I will give them Canaan and I will be your God.
CHORUS *(echoing)*	Yahweh will be your God.
YAHWEH	Sarah will bear a son You are to name him Isaac. I will make him into a great nation.
CHORUS *(echoing)*	A great nation.

(normal)	Sarah bore Isaac, son of Abraham. Count the stars if you can. So shall your descendants be, Abraham, father of many nations. But first your faith must be tried.
YAHWEH	Abraham, Abraham. Take your son, your only child Isaac, whom you love. Offer him on a mountain that I will point out to you.
SOLO 1	How can there be descendants?
SOLO 2	How can there be kings?
SOLO 3	How can there be blessings?
CHORUS	If Isaac is killed? But Abraham went to the mountain with Isaac.
ISAAC *(high voices)*	Father, here are the fire and the wood, but where is the sheep for the offering?
ABRAHAM *(slow, sad)*	My son, God will provide the sheep.
CHORUS *(growing in momentum and intensity)*	Abraham built an altar and arranged the wood. He tied Isaac and laid him on the altar. He reached for the knife to kill his son.
YAHWEH *(loudly)* *(gently)* *(growing in power)*	Abraham. Abraham. Do not harm your boy. I know how devoted you are to me. I will bless you and make your descendants as countless as the stars of the sky and the sands of the seashore. And in your descendants all the nations of the earth shall find blessing.
CHORUS *(peacefully)*	Abraham offered a ram in place of Isaac. Isaac lived to be the father of princes. His descendants were as countless as the stars. And all the nations of the earth were blessed through Abraham, the father of believers.

abcdefghijkl

mnopqrstuv

wxyz AABC

DEEFGHIIJ

KLMNNOP

QRSTTUV

WXYZ

Genesis According to Room 21

ADAM	Hey, Eve, isn't this a nice place to live?
EVE	Sure is, Adam. Whatcha say we have a little snack?
ADAM	Sure. What's your choice? We can eat anything we want.
EVE	Except the apples on that tree over there.
ADAM	Oh, yeah. I forgot. Too bad. They look pretty good.
EVE	They sure do. How about having just one? One couldn't hurt.
ADAM	Yeah, but Eve, the Maker said to leave that tree alone. Anyway, there's a lot of other things we can eat. Here, eat this peach. It looks juicy and sweet.
EVE	Thanks a lot, Adam. Slurp. Hey, you're right. It is pretty good. Hey, Adam, look at that snake in the apple tree over there.
ADAM	Get away, Eve. It might be poisonous.
EVE	Oh, get out. It's only a harmless little snake. Couldn't hurt a fly.
ADAM	Maybe not a fly, but it can hurt you. Now get away.
SNAKE	Don't be afraid. She's right. I couldn't hurt a fly.
EVE	Adam, are you playing some kind of joke on me?
ADAM	Joke? Are you kidding? This ain't no joke.
SNAKE	Hey, guys, so I talk. What's the big deal? I just came to tell you how great the apples are. Why don't you try one?
ADAM	Because the Maker told us not to.
EVE	And anyway there are other trees.
SNAKE	That's not the point. The point is why let him boss you around. You don't have to take that. Go ahead. Enjoy an apple.
EVE	Yeah, why not? Snap. Crunch. Yum. These apples are great. Have a bite, Adam?
ADAM	Yeah, why not? Slurp. Hey, we better get some clothes on. Here, wear this.
EVE	Thanks. You know, Adam, we've been tricked.
ADAM	I know.
GOD	This way to the exit, folks.

Study Guide for the
Constitution on Divine Revelation

Prologue

1 Why did the Synod write this document? (It wants the whole world to hear the summons to salvation, so that through hearing it may believe, through belief it may hope, through hope it may come to love.)

Divine Revelation Itself

2 What was God's will revealed to us? (That people should have access to the Father, through Christ, the Word made flesh, in the Holy Spirit, and thus become sharers in the divine nature.); Who is the mediator and sum total of Revelation? (Christ)

3 What gives us evidence of God? (Created realities); What promise did God reveal through the ages? (The promise of redemption)

4 What did Jesus reveal about God? (The inner life of God; God was with us to deliver us from the darkness of sin and death, and to raise us up to eternal life.)

5 Who perfects our faith and helps us understand Revelation? (The Holy Spirit)

6 How does Revelation aid reason? (Things beyond reason can be known by all with ease, with firm certainty, and without the contamination of error.)

The Translation of Divine Revelation

7 Who handed on the Gospel? (The apostles); Who are their successors? (Bishops); What is the mirror in which we see God? (Tradition and the Scripture of both Testaments)

8 What does the apostolic tradition comprise? (Everything that serves to make the people of God live their lives in holiness and increase their faith); In what sense does Tradition make progress in the Church? (There is a growth in insight into the realities and words that are being passed on. The Church advances toward the plenitude of divine truth.)

9 Where is the Word of God found? (Scripture and Tradition)

10 Who is entrusted with interpreting the Word of God? (The living teaching office of the Church alone)

73

Sacred Scripture: Its Divine Inspiration and Its Interpretation

11   Why are all biblical books sacred and canonical? (Written under the inspiration of the Holy Spirit, they have God for their author.); What truth does Scripture teach? (The truth which God wished to see confided to it)

12   What must the interpreters of Scripture do? (Search out the meaning which the sacred writers had in mind); What must interpreting Scripture take into account? (Literary forms, patterns of perception, speech and narrative which prevailed at the time of the sacred writers; the conventions which the people of this time followed in their dealing with one another; the Tradition of the entire Church)

13   What can the word of God in the human languages be compared to? (The Word of the eternal Father become man)

The Old Testament

14   Through what people did God first entrust his promises? (Israel)

15   Why are the Hebrew Scriptures valuable? (They prophecy Christ, provide an understanding of God and his dealings with people, show authentic divine teaching and are a treasury of prayer.)

16   Where does the Old Testament find full meaning? (The New Testament)

The New Testament

17   Why do the Gospels have a special place? (They are our principal source for the life and teaching of the Incarnate Word, our Savior.)

18   What was the purpose of the writers of the Gospels? (That we might know the truth about what Jesus said and did)

19   What do the other New Testament books do? (Firmly establish those matters which concern Christ the Lord, formulate more precisely his authentic teaching, preach the saving power of Christ's divine work and foretell its glorious consummation)

Sacred Scripture in the Life of the Church

20   What should the preaching of the Church and the entire Christian religion be nourished and ruled by? (Sacred Scripture)

21   What does Scripture do for the People of God? (Enlightens the mind, strengthens the will and fires the hearts of people with the love of God)

22   What is the relationship of Scripture to theology? (It is its soul and, together with Tradition, its permanent foundation.)

23   Who should read Scripture? (Clerics, priests, and others who, as deacons or catechists, are officially engaged in the ministry of the Word; all the

Christian faithful, especially those who live the religious life); What should accompany the reading of Scripture? (Prayer)

24 What will increased veneration of the Word of God bring about? (A new impulse of spiritual life)

Note: A helpful reference to books and audiovisuals on the Bible is *Bible Readings and Studies, A Pastoral Bibliography* published by the Publications Office of the United States Catholic Conference, 1312 Massachusetts Ave. N.W., Washington, D.C. 20005.

Illustration I

Jesse Tree Symbols

Apple with two bites out of it (Adam and Eve)
Ark, rainbow, dove carrying a branch (Noah)
Sword of sacrifice (Abraham)
Bundle of wood, lamb in a bush (Isaac)
Pitcher (Rebecca)
Ladder, well (Jacob)
Coat of many colors (Joseph)
Burning bush, tablets of the Law (Moses)
Lamb on the altar (Levi)
Sheaf of wheat (Ruth)
Harp, crown (David)
Temple (Solomon)
Sword (Judith)
Whale (Jonah)
Scroll (Isaiah)
Six-pointed star and chain (Esther)
Baptismal shell (John the Baptizer)
Carpenter's tools, staff (St. Joseph)
Lily, decorated M (Mary)
City of Bethlehem, rising sun, key of David

(See Illustration J)

Jesse Tree

Dance Movements to the Our Father
(Circle Formation)

Our Father
(Hold hands and walk in a circle.)

Who art in heaven
(Raise hands.)

Hallowed be Thy name.
(Fold hands in prayer.)

Thy kingdom come
(Sweep right arm back.)

Thy will be done.
(Bow head and cross arms putting hands on shoulders.)

On earth
(Gesture down with left hand.)

As it is in heaven.
(Gesture up with right hand.)

Give us this day our daily bread
(Cup hand in front as for receiving Holy Communion.)

And forgive us our trespasses
(Kneel on right knee, strike breast and bow head.)

As we forgive those who trespass against us.
(Join hands as you rise. Walk in a circle.)

And lead us not into temptation
(Turn out from circle and shield face.)

But deliver us from evil.
(Extend arms out in front.)

Amen.
(Fold hands. Bow head.)

Illustration L

Kineposium Group Placement Cards

1 SECRETARY 1	**2** 1 2 3 4 5	**3** 2 4 1 3 5	**4** 3 1 4 2 5	**5** 4 3 2 1 5
6 SECRETARY 2	**7** 1 3 5 2 4	**8** 2 5 3 1 4	**9** 3 2 1 5 4	**10** 5 1 2 3 4
11 SECRETARY 3	**12** 1 4 2 5 3	**13** 2 1 5 4 3	**14** 4 5 1 2 3	**15** 5 2 4 1 3
16 SECRETARY 4	**17** 1 5 4 3 2	**18** 3 4 5 1 2	**19** 4 2 5 3 1	**20** 5 3 1 4 2
21 SECRETARY 5	**22** 2 3 4 5 1	**23** 3 5 2 4 1	**24** 4 1 3 5 2	**25** 5 4 3 2 1

Biblical Poems

Concrete poems in which the words shape the message

```
        WHOEVER                    LOVE    LOVE
       WISHES  TO                LOVELOV  LOVELOV
      BE MY FOLLOWER            VELOVELOVEHATELOV
   MUST DENY HIS VERY           LOVELOVELOVELOVEL
    SELF, TAKE UP HIS            ELOVELOVELOVELO
     CROSS EACH DAY                 VELOVELOVEL
      AND FOLLOW IN                  LOVELOVEL
       MY STEPS.                      LOVEL
        WHOEVER                        LOV
       WOULD SAVE                       L
        HIS LIFE
       WILL LOSE                  Matthew 6:43-48
    IT, AND WHO-
    EVER LOSES
       HIS LIFE
    FOR MY SAKE
     WILL SAVE
         IT.
```

Luke 9:23-24

Cinquains

Line 1:   1 word that names the topic
Line 2:   2 words that define or describe the topic
Line 3:   3 words that express action about the topic
Line 4:   4 words that express feeling about the topic
Line 5:   1 word that is a synonym for the topic

Example: Judith
           Lovely, holy
           Conquering the enemy
           Courageous through her faith
           Heroine.

Diamantes (diamond-shaped)

Line 1: 1 word naming the topic.
Line 2: 2 words describing the topic
Line 3: 3 participles (-ing or -ed words) describing the topic
Line 4: 4 words, the first two refer to line one, the second two,
 to the last line (or somehow using the two opposing ideas)
Line 5: 3 participles describing the word in line 7
Line 6: 2 words describing the word in line 7
Line 7: 1 word which is the opposite of the word in line 1
(Hint: Compose the first and last lines first.)

Example:

Sinner
Town prostitute
Longing, selling, crying
She encounters divine love.
Learning, laughing, giving
Jesus' disciple
Saint

Free Verse

Limericks: See Donald R. Bensen's *Biblical Limericks,* published in 1986,
 which is composed entirely of limericks on the Old Testament.

A Sample Meditation

(Zacchaeus - Luke 19:1-10)

Still yourself. Put everything away. Relax. Close your eyes.

Quiet your mind. Empty it of all thoughts and concerns about what you are having for lunch today or what you will do after school. Concentrate on God. God is here now, loving you. God is going to communicate a message that has particular meaning for you.

Reading: Luke 19:1-10

Recreate: Consider Zacchaeus, the wealthy tax collector, a VIP. He is probably a pompous, bossy man. Perhaps he is overweight. He is not well liked. People know he lines his pockets with money stolen from them. Although Zacchaeus is a bigshot, he is short. This is his handicap. Maybe it even makes him defensive and tough. But one day Zacchaeus has an encounter that changes his life.

At first he is only curious to see a popular preacher. After straining in vain to look over the shoulders of the taller members of the crowd, he runs ahead and climbs up a tree. How ridiculous: a fat little official hiding in a tree because of his weakness. But from his perch, Zacchaeus can see. In fact he gets to see more than he planned to. As Jesus passes below, he glances up and searches out Zacchaeus among the leaves. Jesus reveals his secret: He knows other secrets, too. He doesn't scold Zacchaeus or laugh at him. Rather, he honors him. He invites him into further friendship with him. Out of all the people in the crowd, it is Zacchaeus Jesus singles out, and he handles him with gentleness. Zacchaeus scrambles down out of the tree, maybe with a hand from Jesus, and he gives the proper response. He is delighted. Now that Jesus will dine at his house, Zacchaeus feels six feet tall. He is thrilled that Jesus did not wait for an invitation, but presumed on his hospitality, trusted him.

The crowd mutters that Jesus has gone to a sinner's house. Zacchaeus does have a reputation. After dining with Jesus, Zacchaeus stands before his family and guests and admits his sin. Then he is really big. He promises the Lord to change, and he offers to make up in a fitting way: greed is his fault; his remedy will be generosity. Salvation comes to all who welcomed God that day. The crowd, too, would benefit from Zacchaeus' conversion.

Reflect: Let us reflect on this story. Each of us, like Zacchaeus, has shortcomings, weaknesses. Some we can't help—like having a crooked nose or a funny voice. Some we are more responsible for—like being short-tempered or short-sighted. As long as we try to keep our eyes on Jesus, even to the point of acting like a clown, being up a tree and out on a limb, there is hope. But we must be honest with ourselves. We might not have a crowd to point out our faults. But probably we have someone who hints at the thing about us that makes us squirm.

Jesus dwells within us. He says, "I like you, no matter what." We don't have to earn his love. He invites us to dine at Eucharist with him, everyday *if* we wish. The strength of our friendship with Jesus is sufficient power to effect a change in us. He doesn't give up on us when we fail. He encourages us like a mother or father teaching a child to walk. We don't have to hide. He comes for sinners like us. We can be open and stand tall.

Respond: Let us respond to this reading. In the presence of Jesus, look at the way you are living. What is your handicap, your shortcoming? How can you repair it? Ask Jesus to help you. Thank him for his loving care that always seeks out the sinner. [Pause]

Let us respond now with the verse we say at the end of the sacrament of Reconciliation: Give thanks to the Lord for he is good. . . .(His mercy endures forever.)

(It's always a good idea to bring students out of a meditation gradually, using a short vocal prayer as a transition.)

A Seder Meal

(Candles should be lit.)

LEADER   Blessed are you, Lord God, King of the Universe. In love you have chosen us for your service and made us holy through your commandments. You have kept us safe and brought us to this holy season.

ALL   Amen.

LEADER   Let us pour the first cup of wine. *(Raises the cup.)* Blessed are you, Lord God, for this fruit of the vine. Continue to show your love.

ALL   Praise to you, Lord God, Ruler of the World. *(Drink from the cups.)*

LEADER   Let us now dip our herbs.

(All dip parsley or lettuce in salt water and put it on their plates.)

LEADER   Let us pray.

ALL   Praised are you, Lord God, King of the Universe, Creator of the fruit of the earth.

(The greens are eaten.)

LEADER   *(Breaks a piece of matzoh and lifts it.)* This is the poor bread that our ancestors ate in Egypt. Let anyone who is hungry celebrate Passover with us.

ALL   God showed his love for us; we wish to share love with others.

(The youngest persons present ask the following four questions.)

ONE   Why is this night different from all other nights? On this night we eat bread without yeast in it. Why this evening do we eat unleavened bread?

LEADER   In their hurry to leave Egypt, our ancestors had no time to wait for bread to rise, so they made bread without yeast.

TWO   On other nights we eat all types of vegetables. Why tonight do we eat bitter herbs?

LEADER   The herbs remind us of the bitter times in Egypt when we were slaves.

THREE   On all other nights we do not dip greens in salt water. Why on this night do we dip them?

LEADER   We dip greens in salt water to remind us that when we cried, God heard us.

FOUR	Why on this night do we eat reclining?
LEADER	In ancient days to recline at meals was the sign of a free person. We demonstrate our freedom by reclining.

THE PASSOVER STORY

READER	A reading from the Book of Exodus (*Reads Exodus 12:21-28.*)
	(*Now one of the group points to the items on the Seder plate.*)
STUDENT	What is the meaning of the lamb symbolized by the bone?
LEADER	The night when every first born male in the land of Egypt was struck down, homes marked by the blood of the lamb were spared.
STUDENT	What is the meaning of the matzoh?
LEADER	It is the flat bread our ancestors ate in their hurry to leave Egypt.
STUDENT	What is the meaning of the bitter herbs and charoses?
LEADER	They remind us of our hard service and the mortar we had to make for the Egyptians when we were slaves.
ALL	It is our duty to praise and thank God since God brought us from slavery to freedom, from sorrow to joy, from darkness to light.
LEADER	Praise, you servants of the Lord. Praised be the name of the Lord.
ALL	Blessed be the name of the Lord forever.
LEADER	Blessed are you, Lord God, for the fruit of the vine.
ALL	Praise to you, Lord God, Ruler of the World (*Drink from the cup.*)
	(*Matzoh is broken and passed.*)
ALL	Praised are you, Lord God, King of the Universe who made us holy through the commandments and these bitter herbs.
	(*Eat some of the matzoh.*)
	(*Each person receives the horseradish and charoses and places it between two pieces of matzoh.*)
LEADER	Praised are you, Lord God, King of the Universe who made us holy by your commandments and these bitter herbs.
	(*Eat the matzoh. Supper is served at this point.*)

GRACE AFTER MEALS

LEADER	Praised to you, Lord God, King of the Universe who keeps the world with goodness, with grace and with infinite mercy. Your mercy endures forever.
ALL	God, our Father, keep and protect us.

LEADER	Our God, remember us as you remembered our ancestors so that we may find grace, mercy, life, and peace on this feast.
ALL	Amen. *(Drink from the cups.)*
LEADER	May Elijah's spirit enter the hearts of all. May he inspire them to love you, and may he fill them with the desire to build a world with justice and freedom for all.
	(The door is opened for Elijah and then closed.)
LEADER	*(Raises the cup.)* May the Lord bless and keep us.
ALL	Amen.
LEADER	May God's face shine on us.
ALL	Amen.
LEADER	May the Lord grant us peace.
ALL	Amen.
LEADER	Blessed are you, Lord God, for the fruit of the vine. *(Drink from the cups.)*

Bible Bonanza

(Crossword Puzzle)

Illustration P

Across

1. Song-prayers of King David.
6. As punishment, Judah suffered the Babylonian _____ .
10. The God of Israel is _____ God.
11. It gave Samson and Absalom problems.
13. Nickname for the patriarch who doled out Egyptian food.
14. Yahweh will be Israel's God _____ she does as he commands.
16. To understand the Bible one must read _____ .
18. Reluctant prophet to Nineveh.
20. Subject of Ezekiel's vision.
23. Ruth's husband, great-grandfather of David.
24. God's dwelling on earth.
25. Equal to man.
26. Abbreviation for the book of the Law.

Down

2. Jacob had twelve _____ .
3. _____ Israelite is a descendant of Israel (Jacob).
4. Jacob's first wife.
5. An early holy shrine city.
7. The kind of den Daniel was thrown into.
8. Someone who shares the same faith as the Israelites.
9. What Eve was made from.
12. The ark and the Temple were _____ the holy city of Jerusalem.
13. Angels went up and down _____ ladder.
15. Number symbolizing purification.
17. Almost sacrificed by his father.
19. David's best friend.
21. Prophet who attacked Baal and went up in a flaming chariot.

92

27. Prophet who comforts through the idea of the suffering servant.
28. Man of patience in suffering.
29. Heroes during the Syrian persecution.
31. Abbreviation for the part of the Bible containing Hebrew Writings.
33. Prophet who anointed two kings
36. Isaac's wife (modern spelling).
38. Abbreviation for the first book.
40. First murderer.
41. What Solomon called Bathsheba.
42. Number of tribes in the Northern Kingdom of Israel.
43. Moses' sister.
45. Mountain of God for Moses.
47. Israel was _____ to make idols.
48. Keeper of sycamores who violently attacked social injustice.
50. Twin who gave away his birthright.
54. Moses' priest-brother and spokesman.
55. Book containing the story of creation.
58. The father of believers, covenant-partner with God.
60. Abbreviation for a very holy person.
61. Great saving event of Jewish history.
62. The priests here were killed by Saul for sheltering David.
65. One uncomfortable quality of the desert.
67. "The Lord _____ my shepherd."
68. Jacob's father-in-law.
70. God's saving love is for the whole human _____ .
71. Helped Tobit and Jonah.
72. The uncreated Spirit who created the universe.
73. What Saul became due to pride and jealousy.
75. Another name for prophet.
76. Abraham's nephew.
77. A delinquent priest-father that Samuel had to rebuke.
78. A rainbow appeared _____ Noah's flood.
79. City destroyed for its wickedness.
80. The three men in the furnace prayed, "Cold and _____ , bless the Lord."
83. What God answered when Job challenged him with a speech declaring his innocence.
84. Southern kingdom named for the Messiah's tribe.
86. Bread from heaven in the desert.
88. God made the Reed Sea _____ for the Israelites.
89. Solomon's greatest achievement.
90. Abraham's descendants would be as numerous as the _____ .

22. Priest-scribe who founded Judaism by calling Israel back to the Law.
23. Pagan God of Ahab and Jezebel.
25. Prophet's prediction for sinful Israel.
28. Prophet of the exile who was a suffering servant.
30. Killed by his brother.
32. Agreement between God and Israel.
34. The _____ of the northern tribes to the southern tribes was ten to two.
35. God guided his people through the desert as a pillar of _____ .
37. The Promised Land.
38. Goliath was one.
39. Revealed by God to Moses.
43. Two letters that tell how Noah found the earth after the flood.
44. Israel's great liberator and lawgiver.
46. What David didn't need to conquer Goliath.
49. Biblical number of days for creation.
51. First king of Israel.
52. David's rebellious son.
53. Abraham's hometown.
56. Hebrew Queen of Persia who saved her people.
57. King known for his wisdom and wealth.
59. The first man.
63. Famous tower of many languages.
64. People who preserved the promise of a savior.
65. What the Israelites interpreted as the means of God's direct intervention.
66. His marriage symbolized Israel's relationship with Yahweh.
69. David's prophet.
74. King who sinned and repented.
76. Describes Ruth.
81. Abbreviation for the book about the lovely widow who cut off Holofernes' head.
82. Amos called the wealthy ladies _____ cows.
83. Originally occurred in Eden and resulted in the Fall.
85. God predicted to Satan, "_____ will strike at your head."
87. The judge Gideon fought with only 300 men _____ a sign of God's power.

Answers to Bible Bonanza

The completed crossword grid reads:

Row 1: ¹PSALMS ⁶EXILE ⁸M
Row 2: ⁹R ¹⁰ONE ¹¹HA¹²IR I ¹³JOE
Row 3: ¹⁴I¹⁵F N A IT ¹⁷I ¹⁸JONAH ¹⁹J
Row 4: ²⁰BONES ²¹H L ²²E S N C O
Row 5: R L ²³BOAZ ²⁴ARK ²⁵WOMAN
Row 6: ²⁶T ²⁷ISAIAH R A ²⁸JOB A
Row 7: Y J A ²⁹MACCA³⁰BEES ³¹O T
Row 8: ³²C ³³SAMUEL B R ³⁴R H
Row 9: O H ³⁵F ³⁶REBE³⁷CCA A
Row 10: V ³⁸G³⁹N ⁴⁰CAIN L ⁴¹M ⁴²TEN
Row 11: E ⁴³MIRIA⁴⁴M R ⁴⁵SINAI ⁴⁶I
Row 12: ⁴⁷NOT ⁴⁸AMOS ⁴⁹S ⁵⁰E⁵¹S⁵²A⁵³U ⁵⁴AARON
Row 13: A ⁵⁵GE⁵⁶NESIS ⁵⁷S ⁵⁸ABR⁵⁹AHAM
Row 14: N ⁶⁰ST ⁶¹EXODUS D ⁶²NO⁶³B ⁶⁴J
Row 15: T ⁶⁵H⁶⁶OT ⁶⁷IS L ⁶⁸LABAN ⁶⁹R ⁷⁰RACE
Row 16: ⁷¹FISH ⁷²GOD L ⁷³MAD B W
Row 17: ⁷⁴D ⁷⁵SEER M ⁷⁶LOT T ⁷⁷ELI
Row 18: ⁷⁸AFTER ⁷⁹SODOM ⁸⁰CHILL S
Row 19: V O ⁸¹J ⁸²F N Y A ⁸³SH
Row 20: I R ⁸⁴JUDAH ⁸⁵A ⁸⁶MANN⁸⁷A I
Row 21: ⁸⁸DRY D ⁸⁹TEMPLE ⁹⁰SAND

Jonah Filmstrip

Overhead Presentation
on Creation

Prayer Service: The Word of God

Opening Song

LEADER   Lord, we praise and thank you for the gift of your Word. Through it we come to know your goodness and your love for us. Through it we find the way to happiness in this world and the next. Help us to respond to your Word wholeheartedly.

Psalm 119   (Alternate sides)

Side 1   My heart stands in awe at your word. (v. 161)
Side 2   Your word, O LORD, endures forever;
           it is firm as the heavens. (v. 89)

Side 1   I trust in your words. (v. 42)
Side 2   A lamp to my feet is your word
           a light to my path. (v. 105)

Side 1   I will not forget your words. (v. 16)
Side 2   Of your kindness, O LORD, the earth is full
           (v. 64)

Side 1   My soul pines for your salvation;
           I hope in your word. (v. 81)
Side 2   Be good to your servant that I may live
           and keep your words. (v. 17)

READING   Matthew 7:24-27

Time for Reflection

Response   *We praise you, Lord.*

For your Word that reveals you. . .
For your Word that teaches us. . .
For your Word that guides our lives. . .
For your Word that speaks to our hearts. . .
For your Word that lifts our minds to you. . .
For your Word that assures us of your love. . .

Response   *Make us open to your Word, Lord.*

That we may let your Word touch our hearts. . .
That we may grow in understanding of your Word. . .
That we may live by your Word. . .
That we may bring others to know and love your Word. . .
that we may appreciate your goodness in giving us your Word. . .

Closing Song

Additional Ways to Lead Students into Scripture

Additional Ways to Lead Students into Scripture

About the Author

Sister Mary Kathleen Glavich, a Sister of Notre Dame, is editor and author of *Christ Our Life* religion series, published by Loyola University Press. She also teaches eleventh-grade religion at Regina High School in South Euclid, Ohio, and is a sixth-grade catechist at St. Gregory the Great Parish in South Euclid. She has had classroom experience at every grade level, except fourth, and has taught in Catholic Schools and parish religion programs for over 17 years. In her work as editor and author, she has spent a considerable amount of time researching Scripture and Scripture-related resources. In her own words, teaching is her first love. Through this book, her fondest hope is to motivate other teachers and catechists to love teaching—and especially to love leading students into Scripture.